Write Your Own Pleasure Prescription

Dear Mr. Pearsall:

I've read The Pleasure Prescription, *and thanks to you I now know more clearly than ever what I have to do for my family and myself if we are to enjoy life and be healthy together. We're just not sure how to put the principles from your book into practice here on the mainland. Unless you want to send us tickets to Hawaii, we need to know how to use your principles from paradise here in Pittsburgh. Can you send us a bunch of pleasure prescriptions based on your book that we can use to put your ideas into practice in our life?*

A New Polynesian in Pittsburgh

Dear New Polynesian in Pittsburgh:

Mahalo nui (many thanks) for your kind letter. Paradise is not a place to go; it is a way of being. Hawaii is a magical and joyful place not because of its beautiful scenery and temperate climate but because of the ancient lessons of the blissfully happy people who made their home there. I will try to come up with suggestions to help you design your own ticket to paradise. Me ke aloha pumehana (with the very warmest regards).

Dr. Paul Pearsall

Bestselling author and psychologist Paul Pearsall offers 60 new prescriptions for making the spirit of aloha a part of life for readers all over the world. In his inimitable, light-hearted style, he shows that happiness is not a light at the end of the tunnel but a consciousness that allows each of us to take pleasure in the good things in our lives every day. In *Write Your Own Pleasure Prescription*, Pearsall shows readers how to slow down, feel deeply connected to others, and experience the delight that unifies us with the world around us.

For my *Makuahine*,
my mother Carol,
for my *ola*,
my life

Write Your Own Pleasure Prescription

60 Ways to Create
Balance & Joy
in Your Life

Paul Pearsall, Ph.D.

Hunter House PUBLISHERS

For further information contact:
Hunter House Inc., Publishers
P.O. Box 2914
Alameda, CA 94501-0914

Library of Congress Cataloging-in-Publication Data
Pearsall, Paul.
Write your own pleasure prescription : 60 ways to create balance and joy in your life / by Paul Pearsall. — 1st ed.
p. cm.
ISBN 0-89793-229-3 (pbk.)
1. Pleasure. 2. Stress management. 3. Conduct of life. 4. Polynesia—Social life and customs. I. Title.
BF515.P33 1997
152.4'2—dc21   97-18265
CIP

Cover Design: MIG/Design Works   Book design: Martha Blegen
Editorial Coordinator: Dana Weissman, Belinda Breyer
Production Coordinator: Wendy Low
Editor: Laura Harger
Sales & Marketing: Corrine M. Sahli   Marketing Associate: Susan Markey
Customer Service: Christina Arciniega, Edgar M. Estavilla, Jr.
Business Management: Mike Nealy
Fulfillment: A & A Quality Shipping
Publisher: Kiran S. Rana

Printed and bound by Publishers Press, Salt Lake City UT
Manufactured in the United States of America

9 8 7 6 5 4 3 2 1 First edition

OTHER BOOKS AND AUDIOTAPES BY PAUL PEARSALL, PH.D.

Superimmunity: Master Your Emotions and Improve Your Health

Super Marital Sex: Loving for Life

Super Joy: Learning to Celebrate Everyday Life

The Power of the Family: Strength, Comfort, and Healing

Making Miracles

The Ten Laws of Lasting Love

A Healing Intimacy: The Power of Loving Connections

The Pleasure Prescription: To Love, to Work, to Play—Life in the Balance

The Pleasure Prescription (On audiotape)

The Heart's Code: New Findings About Cellular Memories and their Role in the Mind, Body, Spirit Connection (April 1998)

Contents

Contents

Important Note for the Reader

The material in this book is intended to provide an overview of the health and healing implications of the traditions and practices of Polynesian cultures and related scientific and medical research, especially in the field of psychoneuroimmunology (PNI). Such research is referenced both in this book and in its companion book, *The Pleasure Prescription*, for those readers wishing to make further inquiries. Every effort has been made to provide accurate and dependable information. However, the reader should be aware that professionals may have differing opinions about the implications of research, and change is always taking place. Any suggestions for techniques, treatments, or lifestyle changes described in this book should be used under the guidance of a licensed therapist or health-care practitioner. The author, editors, and publisher cannot be held responsible for any outcomes of trying the ideas and suggestions in this book in a program of self-care or under the care of a licensed professional. The ideas, suggestions, and techniques in this book should not be used in place of other medical therapies.

Acknowledgments

Hoʻi hou i ka mole
Pronounced "ho-ee ho-oo ee ka moh-lay"

To remember one's foundation, symbolized by the root of the *kalo* (taro) plant, the source of all physical and spiritual subsistence and the symbol of family in Hawaiʻi

In Hawaiʻi, there is nothing more sacred than the *'ohana* (family). The word *po'ohala* means to perpetuate one's basic family virtues, the five components of *aloha* that have served as the foundation for *The Pleasure Prescription* and this book as well. I learned the virtues of *aloha* from the *kanaka maoli* (people of Hawaiʻi), and I give them my most profound *mahalo* (thanks). Mahalo to my Hawaiʻi *'ohana*, whom I named in my dedication to *The Pleasure Prescription*. I apologize to them and to all Hawaiians for any mistakes I've made in trying to convey their wisdom, and I promise that I will keep trying to learn their most profound and enduring lessons about living, working, loving, and playing in *pono*—"righteous balance."

I give my *kipona aloha* (deepest love) to my wife, Celest, without whose *mana* (energy) I would not be alive to write this book. *(Me ke aloha ku'uipo Kalalani.)* My *kipona aloha* to my sons, Roger and Scott, who will always be my ultimate source of pride and joy. *Mahalo* to my brother Dennis, his wife, Sandy, and my nephew and nieces for extending the *aloha* of our *'ohana*. As always, my *kipona aloha* to my father, Frank, whose *mana* is forever within me.

All books are *'ohana*-made. Like the navigator on the canoe, the author is only a part of this crew. I give my *aloha* to my publishing *'ohana* at Hunter House, a small but sturdy canoe in the large and often rough seas of publishing. *Mahalo* to my publisher, Kiran Rana, for sharing my *mana'o* (ideas) and being attuned to and willing to publish a book written from my *na'au* (spiritual center). *Mahalo nui* to marketing director Corrine Sahli for doing much more than anyone has a right to expect and for doing it so very well. *Mahalo* to my editor, Laura Harger, who worked so patiently, diligently, and creatively to help shape a book that shares just some of the *mana'o* from paradise.

Preface

When my book *The Pleasure Prescription: To Love, to Work, to Play—Life in the Balance* hit the best-seller lists, I received hundreds of letters. One of these letters illustrates the need expressed in most of this correspondence.

"Dear Dr. Pearsall: I've read your book, and thanks to you I now know more clearly than ever what I have to do for my family and myself if we are to enjoy life and be healthy together. We're just not sure *how* to put the principles from your book into practice here on the mainland. Unless you want to send us a ticket to Hawai'i, we need to know how to use your principles from paradise here in Pittsburgh. Can you send us a bunch of pleasure prescriptions based on your book that we can use to put your ideas into practice in our real life, and have a lot of *aloha* in the Midwest?"

—*A New Polynesian in Pittsburgh*

Here was my answer to this letter:

"Dear New Polynesian in Pittsburgh: *Mahalo nui* (many thanks) for your kind letter. Paradise is not a place to go; it is a way of being. Hawai'i is a magical and joyful place not because of its beautiful scenery and temperate climate, but because of the ancient lessons of the blissfully happy people who make their home there.

"I will try to come up with suggestions to help you design your own ticket to paradise. *Me ke aloha pumehana* (with the very warmest regards)!"

—*Dr. Paul Pearsall*

This manual is my answer to the Polynesian in Pittsburgh and to everyone who wants to learn how to reawaken to the enchantment of their own life, no matter where they live. It's intended to give you some ideas for crafting your own ticket to your own paradise right where you live, work, love, and play. It's designed to teach you how to combine the ancient wisdom of Polynesia with the best modern medical research in practical prescriptions for healthy balance, complete connection—with yourself, your loved ones, and your world—and more delight in your and your family's daily loving, working, playing, and healing.

This is a companion book to *The Pleasure Prescription* and a key to putting the principles of pleasure, as explained in that book, to work in your life. You can use this "joy book" in conjunction with *The Pleasure Prescription* or on its own as a way to begin exploring paradise. This book offers you a review of and more information on the pleasure principles of Polynesia and gives you a variety of new techniques, ideas, exercises, and readings that you can use to begin living the pleasure-filled life. It asks you questions for reflection and it asks you to do some writing of your own about pleasure. It teaches you new skills and aptitudes for pleasure and offers you "pleasure prescriptions"—practical action plans for bringing joy into your life—that will launch you on a long, blissful cruise toward the paradise that life promises us all.

It will be very helpful to you if, before reading through this book, you've read *The Pleasure Prescription,* in which you can learn more about the principles of *aloha* and discover how the most recent medical research is substantiating Polynesia's ancient lessons of joy and well-being. However, if you are feeling strapped for time—if you're feeling the stress and pressure characteristic of our Western way of life—you may want to begin with this book as a form of CPR, cheerful pleasure relief, and turn to *The Pleasure Prescription* later.

Introduction

Are You a Pleasure?

'Ano'ai ke aloha
Pronounced "ah-no ah-ee kay ah-lo-ha"

Greetings of love

While we can't all board the next plane for Hawai'i, we can use the teachings of Polynesian wisdom to improve our lives here and now. Polynesia, meaning the huge complex of islands and archipelagos that stretches across the southern Pacific, is home to a unique set of teachings about the ways people think and live. Distinctly different from the Western ideal of life (in which each person is taught to be self-sufficient and told to focus on self-fulfillment) and from the Eastern ideal of life (which emphasizes the quest for enlightenment), the Polynesian or Oceanic Way teaches that a joyful and healthy life is based on embracing life by sharing its sacredness and its pleasure with others. Teaching patience instead of urgency, working together instead of working against one another, and living in connection with the earth rather than in control of it, the Polynesian Way—based on the principles of *aloha*—offers us a powerful prescription for bringing pleasure and bliss into our lives.

Living *Aloha*

Before learning to write and use pleasure prescriptions—before you can put the teachings of Polynesian wisdom to work in your life—you'll need to understand *aloha*. *Aloha* means many things, including "love," "sacred breath," "hello," and "goodbye," but the word itself also contains the philosophical foundations of life in Polynesia: A, *ahonui*; L, *lokahi*; O, *'olu'olu*; H, *ha'aha'a*; and A, *akahai*. Each of these five *aloha* principles carries an important lesson for pleasure-prescription writing. Let's briefly review them in turn.

Ahonui (pronounced "ah-ho-new-ee")—Patience, Expressed with Perseverance. Meaning "the great breath," *ahonui* expresses the Polynesian belief that patience is the breath of life. A patient person is a person who is calm enough to fully connect with herself, her loved ones, and her world, breathing in all of existence.

    Ahonui is essential for pleasure-prescription writing because it's essential to living a balanced and healthful life. *Ahonui* reminds us to slow down, to live in the present, and to recognize the beauty and joy of life right now.

Lokahi (pronounced "low-ka-hee")—Unity, Expressed Harmoniously. *Lokahi*, meaning "unity," expresses the importance of living in connection with the earth and with others. Polynesians recognize that humans live in communities and in nature, and know that we are not single, autonomous units—what we do affects others and affects the earth. *Lokahi* reminds us that in order to enjoy life and remain healthy, we need to feel connected to ourselves, our families, our friends, and our society, and that we need to feel connected to the natural world as well.

'Olu'olu (pronounced "oh-lew oh-lew")—Agreeableness, Expressed with Pleasantness. Literally meaning "flexible" or "pliant," *'olu'olu* expresses the importance of congeniality, politeness, and forgiveness to Polynesians. Anger, as I discussed in *The Pleasure Prescription*, is a leading killer—when we get angry, our bodies go into overdrive, straining our hearts and our immune systems. *'Olu'olu* reminds us that anger harms us and those around us. Pleasure is brought into our lives when we learn to live in harmony.

Ha'aha'a (pronounced "ha ah-ha ah")—Humbleness, Expressed with Modesty. Literally meaning "unassuming," *ha'aha'a* reminds us of the importance of humbleness and the dangers of egocentricity. In Polynesia, bragging is considered enormously rude, an assumption of superiority that damages the braggart by distancing her from others and from the world. *Ha'aha'a* reminds us that, contrary to the Western idea that we need to stand on our own and "look out for Number One," a pleasurable life is one lived in connection with others, in which we look out for everyone.

Akahai (pronounced "ah-ka-ha-ee")—Kindness, Expressed with Tenderness. Illustrating the key place of giving and selflessness in Polynesian culture, *akahai* means "gentle caring." Teaching that the world is reciprocal—that as we give, so shall we receive—*akahai* reminds us of the importance of giving to others. When we bring pleasure to others, pleasure returns to us.

Medical research has shown that people who truly enjoy life and who live balanced and pleasurable lives in deep connection with others—as the *aloha* principles teach us to do—are healthier and live longer. The principles of *aloha* also have the power to awaken us to the possibilities of life and show us how we can find deep, lasting, and truly meaningful pleasure. Teaching that pleasure means caring for others and for the world—rather than simply enjoying ourselves—and that pleasure means slowing down and living a balanced life, the *aloha* principles form the basis of the pleasure prescriptions that this book will teach you to use and write.

Before you read further in this book, you may wish to take the *Aloha* Test, which you can find in *The Pleasure Prescription*. The *Aloha* Test can tell you about your levels of *ahonui, lokahi, 'olu'olu, ha'aha'a,* and *akahai,* and suggest to you areas of your life in which you will benefit from writing and using pleasure prescriptions. And as you learn to put pleasure prescriptions to work in your own life, you can return to the *Aloha* Test and take it again to assess your progress and watch your growth in a wonderful new life of *aloha* pleasure.

What Is a Pleasure Prescription?

A pleasure prescription is a way in which we can bring the powerful *aloha* principles to life. Our "seventh sense"—the sense that lives alongside our sight, hearing, taste, touch, smell, and psychic sense—directs us toward healthy, fulfilling, and lasting pleasure and warns us away from what will damage our health and our soul. It causes us to ask what we can do to make life more enjoyable and meaningful.

Pleasure prescriptions are a wonderful way of exercising and fulfilling this seventh sense. A pleasure prescription can be a brief exercise or a long, thought-provoking meditation. A prescription might be scheduling a brief time with your spouse to spend in loving, quiet communication; it might be reconsidering whether your job is truly in harmony with your principles and needs. A pleasure prescription might mean a short walk in which you perceive the beauty of the day or it might mean embarking upon a lifelong process of healing. In its own way, this book itself is a pleasure prescription—as you read through it and absorb its lessons, you are learning to bring healthy pleasure into your life.

In the last sections of this book, you'll read about sixty pleasure prescriptions that you can use to bring *aloha pumehana, aloha hana, aloha pa'ani,* and *aloha lapa'au* (warm loving, loving work, loving play, and healing love) into your life. Each of these prescriptions can help you bring the power of *aloha* and Polynesian wisdom into your life and help you begin to experience the bliss and balance that will truly feed your seventh sense.

As you read through this book and begin to use the pleasure prescriptions, you may start thinking about other prescriptions that you may wish to try—prescriptions written out of your own life and oriented toward the questions that your own seventh sense may be asking you. At the end of the book, we'll discuss ways that you can begin to write prescriptions of your own.

As I mentioned earlier, the five principles of *aloha* form the basis of every prescription in this book. Here is a brief checklist that will help you remember the five *aloha* principles and apply them to your pleasure-prescription learning and writing:

1. *Ahonui:* Be patient. Don't rush yourself. You will never finish this manual because its *aloha* lessons for pleasure-prescription writing are designed both to take a lifetime and to help you find more time for your life.

2. *Lokahi:* Connect. Don't try to go through this book alone. Find someone else—a friend, your spouse, a relative—to serve as your sailing partner on this cruise to a more pleasurable, intimate, balanced life.

3. *'Olu'olu:* Be agreeable and tolerant. Don't get upset and angry with yourself when the sixty pleasure prescriptions and other lessons in this

joy book seem difficult to fill. Treat yourself as a stranger in paradise, trying your best to learn its blissful ways.

4. Ha'aha'a: Be humble. Don't try to "be your very best" or to be better at writing pleasure prescriptions than anyone else. Be modest in your efforts and realize that the real benefit of living *aloha* comes from being willing to take the voyage, not from getting quickly or first to the destination. View your destination as somewhere out on the horizon of the vast ocean, where the sky meets the water, and know that you can never really get there. The beautiful horizon is no less splendid for being a place that one never reaches.

5. Akahai: Finally, don't work too hard at your prescription writing. Be gentle and tender in your learning. Your brain, steeped in Western ideas of self-sufficiency and perfectionism, may mock your attempts to live in *aloha* or may tell you that you aren't working hard enough. Don't listen—and always remember to treat yourself with kindness and patience.

The Most Important Question in the World

This is a book for doing, not just reading, so let's get started. First, consider what the latest research suggests may be the most important question in the world: **Would those who know you best say that you are a total pleasure to live, love, play, and work with?**

Your answer to this question not only helps you begin your journey through this joy book. It also reflects your overall physical and mental health and healing potential, and it can tell you whether you can expect to lead a healthy and pleasurable life. Medical research shows that this question is at least if not more important in determining your healthfulness as such questions as "What do you weigh?" "What do you eat?" "What's your cholesterol count?" "Are you getting enough exercise?"

Ancient Hawaiians knew and modern research is proving that joyful connection with other people and the world in general is one of the strongest predictors of physical, mental, and spiritual health. Happily connected people—people who bring pleasure to those around them and receive pleasure in return—tend to have stronger immune systems: they get sick less and get better more quickly when they are ill. The objective of the pleasure prescriptions you will be writing is more intimate, blissful, and pleasant connection with everyone and everything. So if you can answer a strong, unhesitating "Yes!" to this most important question, your chance and the chances of those around you of living long and well are very good. But even if your answer is "No," don't despair. We can all learn to lead a life that yields a more consistent and stronger "yes," and this book shows you how to do it.

Notice that the question asked here is not whether your life is a pleasure just for you, but whether you are a pleasure to others. Learning to write pleasure prescriptions requires learning different definitions of "your" and "own." It asks you to discover new definitions based on the Oceanic model of a collective and connected self. If you are interested in having it all, doing it all, and being completely self-fulfilled, you have purchased the wrong book. However, if you are interested in discovering the most magnificent and healthy pleasure imaginable—based on learning to want what you have, doing less but enjoying life more, and celebrating the miracle of "us"—you have just bought a map to the joyful treasures of life buried beneath the stress and strain of daily life on Paradise Earth.

Before you begin using and writing pleasure prescriptions, you'll want to test your "pleasure-ability," the amount of pleasure you bring to those around you. (If you're unsure about your answer to the question above, this test may help you focus your mind.) To determine your pleasure-ability, circle the letter below that best applies to you. If you are courageous, have someone at work, at home, and with whom you play score you too.

A: A real gem

Everyone would say that I'm always absolutely wonderful to be around.

B: A treat

Almost everyone would say that I'm nice to be around, but just a few others would say that (on rare occasions) I can be a drag.

C: A challenge

Some people would say that it's pretty nice being with me, but more than a few others would say that being around me too long gets difficult.

D: A pain

Only a very few people would say that they like being with me; many others would say that I'm often no treat to be around.

E: A total pain

Almost everyone would say that I'm a real pain in the neck (or lower)!

If you or someone else graded you C or lower, you need to ponder the first rule of healthy pleasure: Us-fulfillment, not self-fulfillment, is the secret to health and happiness. Despite popular psychology's insistence on self-love, the idea that you must first love yourself before you can love others is pure myth. Polynesia teaches us that we all live in connection—not only with ourselves, but with our families, our communities, and our world. None of us is a lone self, and thus loving is a reciprocal process that does not recognize divisions between the lover and the loved.

Healthy pleasure means healthy loving of life, others, and the world, and it is first and foremost interdependent, not independent. Living a long and joyful life based on *aloha* requires living to make others feel glad they are alive, rather than living only to make your own life happier. You do not have to be a hopelessly codependent martyr in order to dedicate your life to being pleasing, rather than just trying to be pleased: pleasure is reciprocal, and what you give comes back to you. Writing your own pleasure prescriptions requires that you first learn that the way to healthy joy is with and for others.

The Navigator's Tools

As you move through this book, learning to apply *aloha* principles to your life and learning to write and use pleasure prescriptions, you are much like a Polynesian navigator preparing for and undertaking a great journey: the journey of learning to live in true and fulfilling pleasure, in harmony with your seventh sense.

Any wise navigator, before embarking on a trip, gathers together tools that will help her on her voyage. In this section I'll present you with a number of "navigator's tools" that will help you as you read this pleasure-prescription handbook.

The Joy of Moseying: There is a reason why we call ourselves "the human race." We seem caught up in an endless contest with others to "go for it," to get our piece of the pie. In our pursuit of self-pleasure, we rush right past the simple delight of sharing the grit and grace of daily living with others. Remember, as you go through this book, that pleasure prescriptions are not really for you; they aren't things that you do for yourself. They are joyful ways of being with others and the world.

Pleasure prescriptions are not intended to help you fulfill your wildest dreams, but to teach you to tame your brain and to dream gently with others about how to share a more fulfilling life. You end up writing unfillable prescriptions if you are in search of a better life for yourself alone. "Going for it" guarantees only that you will keep going and that you will never be really satisfied or even clear about the "it." Fillable pleasure prescriptions, on the other hand, are based on learning to "be here now" with others.

Take some time before you continue reading and reflect on this idea of us-fulfillment as the path to joyful health. Decide to drop out of the race and learn the pace of healthy, balanced pleasure.

If you can't slow your racing brain to pay attention to the question asked here, try using your body to quiet your brain. Go out for a walk, and walk slowly. Learn to mosey to quiet the mind. Saunter, don't scurry. Ramble, don't rush. Meander, don't march. Stroll, don't speed. Wander rather than whiz to work. Try changing the pace of your physical behavior to teach your Western brain to leave your body alone and to stop shoving and pushing it around and forcing it to be a constantly busy body.

Be aware that, like many assignments in this workbook, moseying takes courage. Many people around you are in a real hurry, so step out of the way and be ready to tolerate their disgusted looks. They have not yet learned to write pleasure prescriptions.

Pleasure Pauses: Stop Reading, Start Reflecting: Many times throughout this book, I will ask you to take a pleasure pause. I will ask you to stop reading, put the book down, and reflect on the ideas behind pleasure-prescription writing. Many of the sixty prescriptions at the end of this book do not require that you do something. They are simply thoughts and ideas for you to reflect upon and contemplate. Just by thinking some new thoughts, you can alter your psychochemicals, moving out of a "stressed" life and reversing those eight letters to enable yo to enjoy the "desserts" of living. But you can't get those desserts by rushing through your learning; their delicious rewards can only be yours through slow and gentle reflection.

Take a pleasure pause now and reflect again on the grade you gave yourself on pleasure-ability and your answer to the question "Would those who know me best say that I am a total pleasure to live, love, play, and work with?" Take your time. This book will probably take a lifetime to finish anyway.

Beware the Pleasure Cynics! Pleasure cynics may be other people or they may be your own "inner cynics." They will often challenge your efforts to live in *aloha*. They will say that such efforts are not normal or realistic. They will say that the ideas of *aloha* are nonsense. They will say that pleasure is something achieved only by hard work and sacrifice, something experienced only during temporary vacations from "real" life.

I'm often asked if I really know anyone who practices the *aloha* principles described in *The Pleasure Prescription* or who grades an A or high B on the pleasure-ability test. I'm asked if I'm being a Pollyanna, impractical, unrealistic, or just plain silly. I'm told that, because I live in Hawai'i, I don't live in the real world. As a student of pleasure-prescription writing, how would you answer such challenges from pleasure cynics or perhaps from your own inner cynic? Take a pleasure pause now and write your answers to these questions before reading my answers.

Do you think the idea of living for healthy, balanced, connected pleasure is unrealistic or impractical? Why?

_____

_____

_____

_____

_____

_____

_____

_____

_____

_____

_____

_____

_____

How do you answer the challenges that come from inner and outer pleasure cynics?

_____

_____

_____

_____

_____

_____

_____

_____

_____

_____

_____

Here are my own answers. I agree that leading a life of shared pleasure is no longer "normal." That's the whole point! Being normal today
is a major risk to your health. I am encouraged that my ideas about
healthy pleasure are called nonsense, because this means that while my
ideas make perfect sense in Polynesia, where pleasure and healthy balance and connection are ways of life, they do not make sense from the
Western brain's selfish, pleasure-starved perspective. We need more of
the healthier, joyful perspective of Oceania, and I believe that we can
gain this perspective not by giving up and running away to live on a
beach, but by learning a new way of living and being in the soul.
Healthy pleasure prescriptions are not written by dropping out, but by
totally tuning in.

Practice your own answers to the pleasure cynics. I promise you that
you will make them very uncomfortable as you learn to write your pleasure prescriptions. Remember that healthy pleasure is shared pleasure,
so try to teach them by example. Don't preach, do. Don't defend,
model. Don't be impatient with your critics. Instead, use their cynicism
as reminders of the joyless living you are enjoying your way out of.

I do know and live with people, and you probably do too, who write
and share their own pleasure prescriptions every day of their lives. Take
another pleasure pause now and write down the names of those people
in your life who grade A on pleasure-ability.

_____

_____

_____

_____

_____

_____

_____

_____

_____

My own list of "pleasure-ers" includes my deceased father, my wife, Celest, my sons, my mother, my brother, and my many friends in Hawai'i. Of course, I am very biased about my own family. They saved my life when I had cancer and underwent a bone-marrow transplant. I know that these people are not perfect, but I also know that they live their lives giving pleasure to get pleasure, rather than in the pursuit of selfish pleasure.

Don't Just Read—Speak Up! Another example of someone who knew how to write pleasure prescriptions was Aunty Edith Kanaka'ole, who wrote the chant (called *oli* in Hawaiian) that I excerpted at the beginning of this introduction. Aunty Edith was one of the most cherished teachers in Hawai'i, a master Hawaiian chanter, composer, poet, dancer, and scholar. I did not know her personally, but I know many of her family members and they have told me about the joy she brought to them and the world. (Hawaiians use the words "aunty" and "uncle" in reverence for people who have brought pleasure to others throughout their long lives, whether or not the person referred to is actually one's own aunt or uncle. Because they are ambassadors of *aloha,* they become everyone's aunties and uncles.) Aunty Edith was a person who knew, taught, and practiced the secrets of healthy pleasure-prescription writing. Among her many legacies is the chant of greetings that set the stage for your Polynesian voyage through this book.

Aunty Edith chanted "*Ano'ai ke aloha ia kakou ah pau loa*" (pronounced "ah-no ah-ee kay ah-lo-ha ee-ah ka-co-oo ah pa-oo low-ah"). This chant means "Greetings of love to be shared among us all." When you speak this *oli,* you collectively welcome and share the joy of every day of your life with those you love; you bask in awe at the privilege of being alive; you celebrate and share the sacred breath of life. Begin your pleasure-prescription course right now by trying to sense the joyful *mana* (energy) that can come from chanting these ancient Polynesian words (see the exercise on page 14).

Throughout this book, I will not only be asking you to stop reading and take pleasure pauses. I will also be using Hawaiian words and phrases like Aunty Edith's chant to help you break free of your Western brain's lock on your life. (If you need some help pronouncing the words, turn to Pleasure Prescription Supplement One: *Ho'o Hawai'i* [Speaking a Little Hawaiian] at the end of this book.) I use Polynesian words because I believe, as the Polynesians do, that words have *mana* and have the power to make life a true pleasure. Hawaiians who are able to give and take great pleasure in their lives know that speaking is a way of connecting with the past, present, and future, a way of creating a healing *mana* field. Patient, harmonious, agreeable, humble, and kind words create loving energy waves that resonate in the people and things around the speaker, creating a delight domain and an ecology of pleasure.

One very important lesson for your pleasure-prescription writing is remembering a rule that we often ignore in our hurried life: "Watch your mouth!" Whenever you utter a sound, you have chosen to broadcast your soul. To speak is to convert a part of your *'uhane* (meaning "soul" and pronounced "oo-ha-nay") into sound waves that vibrate with the *'uhane* of everyone around you, the *'aina* (meaning "earth" and pronounced "eye-nah"), and your *na kupuna* (meaning "ancestors" and pronounced "nah koo-poo-nah"). These same waves of *mana* reverberate right back to you. What goes around, comes around.

As often as possible as you go through this book, *'olelo* (speak up)! Read out loud and chant the *oli* that begin many of this book's chapters. These chants have been chosen for their power and beauty. Chanting is a way of "en-chanting" your life and the life of others. It has always been one of the most powerful means of connecting with the meaning of life. Remember, however, that when you chant and speak up that you are never just talking. Every word you utter creates a bond with someone, some place, or some time, so resolve right now to watch your mouth and to speak with *aloha*—patience, unity, agreeableness, humbleness, and kindness.

As you speak up, know that the ancient Polynesian words you will be saying are pretested for your protection and have been proven, over 2,000 years, to bring and give great joy. They are full of historical *na'auao* (meaning "wisdom" and pronounced "nah ah-oo-ah-oh") and are capable of summoning the *aloha* of your ancestors to help soothe you in your times of stress and strain. Also, because the Hawaiian words are probably quite new to you, chanting them aloud will help you slow down in your reading, reflect upon what you've learned, and tune out the chatter of your stressed Western brain.

The Fun of Your First *Oli* (Hawaiian Chant)

Here's how to do your first chant—Aunty Edith's *"'Ano'ai ke aloha ia kakou ah pau loa."*

Stand up, straighten your shoulders, hold this book in front of you to see the words of the chant or write the words on a card, take a deep breath, and begin by pronouncing out loud each one of the syllables of this simple but heartfelt Hawaiian message. Say it slowly, softly, and gently: "Ah-no eye-ee kay ah-lo-ha ee-ah ka-co-oo ah pa-oo low-ah"—"Greetings of love to be shared among us all." Remember as you say these words that you are calling forth your ancestors and inviting them—and the people in your life—to join together with you in loving joy. If you repeat this chant with love several times, you will begin to feel the pleasure of connection flowing within you.

It is impossible to say the syllables of this chant if you are rushing or distracted by your Western brain's interest in doing something else. Think of some place or someone you love, with whom you have shared *aloha,* and say this chant over and over again. Don't worry about getting it "right." Open your heart, take your time, and don't forget to smile as you chant. The more you gently and slowly repeat the sounds—"Ah-no eye-ee kay ah-lo-ha ee-ah ka-cooo ah pa-oo low-ah"—"greetings of love to be shared among us all"—the more your *na kupuna* will help you say these words with patience, unity, agreeableness, humbleness, and kindness. I promise that you will feel *mana* from your *na kupuna* and that they will help you as you learn to write your own prescriptions for a life of healthy pleasure.

The *Aloha* **Alliance:** As you go through this book, I hope you will learn what the people of paradise have known all along—that true pleasure is not self-fulfillment, but complete and deep connection, respect, and caring for everyone, everything, and every time. Pleasure cannot be pursued. Instead, it ensues from being and living in an *aloha* alliance.

The *oli* you have just practiced is a call for an *aloha* alliance. An *aloha* alliance joins us together with the earth, those around us, and the ancestors, and it expresses a profound respect for the past. To form an *aloha* alliance is to form a sacred covenant with everyone and everything around you. It is the constant attempt to think, feel, and behave with the idea of the world's welfare in your heart and the idea of others' joyful living on your mind. An *aloha* alliance is the exact opposite of working for self-fulfillment. It asks us to think about, feel, see, and hear the world as part of the world, and not as users of it. When you have formed your *aloha* alliance, you will use the words *us* and *ours* much more often than *I* and *mine*.

Charting the Course to Pleasure

In order to help you navigate safely and joyfully on your voyage to paradise, I have structured this book into four sections. Always remember that this joy book is intended to be fun, not a struggle.

When you are not having fun, put the book down, take a pleasure pause, and come back to it later. As one *kahuna* (meaning "Hawaiian healer" and pronounced "ka-who-na") told me, "We should not try to paddle our canoe faster just because we are lost. Sometimes we just have to sit and let the canoe take us."

Section One invites you to "change your mind" by learning a Third Way to well-being—the Oceanic Way. It teaches you how to chart for yourself and those around you a more pleasurable life. Chapter One helps you think like the navigator of a Polynesian canoe rather than like a soldier in the daily wars of living. Chapter Two teaches you how to make and take the time to develop a happier, more balanced "in-look" on life. It also presents three very important questions regarding healthy pleasure, three "pleasure prompters" that I invite you to review and answer again after you have read through this entire book. Chapter Three shows you how to catch your breath in an increasingly breathless, fast-paced world. Chapter Four gives you five concepts that you must store away for your voyage of joy, concepts that extend to modern life the five ancient principles of *aloha.*

Just like the Polynesian sailors of centuries ago, any wise sea voyager not only makes sure of where he is going, he is ever mindful of his starting point. Thus, Chapter Five helps you assess your seaworthiness by teaching you to measure your present "pleasure quotient" and "psychoimmunity," two key predictors of your success in living and practicing *aloha.* Chapter Six presents some encouragements and cautions as you begin your journey of joy.

After you have learned to think more like a Polynesian navigator and assessed your seaworthiness for the pleasure voyage, Section Two will teach you the three key aptitudes of a "pleasure-able" person—-wisdom, virtue, and emotional intelligence, discussed in Chapters Seven, Eight, and Nine respectively. Section Two concludes with a summary of the ancient concepts of *aloha* as related to these three key pleasure skills.

Section Three presents sixty prescriptions for pleasure in your loving, working, playing, and healing. Some of these prescriptions call for contemplation, others for chanting and doing, and all for sharing. Finally, your joy book ends by teaching you to write and apply your own prescriptions and suggesting that you and your family *ho'omaka hou*— "begin anew" by committing to a more patient, tender life of shared pleasure.

I've included some learning supplements at the end of this book. Pleasure Prescription Supplement One is called *Ho'o Hawai'i* (Speaking a Little Hawaiian). It helps you learn and practice the sounds of paradise to help bring more pleasure into your life and to help you broadcast your bliss. Pleasure Prescription Supplement Two is a glossary of the Hawaiian words used throughout this book. It can serve as a reminder of the words you have learned and practiced and a brief summary of some the important lessons of *aloha.* Supplement Three is a reading list for those who want to read and study more about the power of pleasure, and who want to try to help all of us awaken to the paradise in which we live.

I hope you will take plenty of time to learn to "en-joy" this manual and to bring joy into your life and the lives of others. I hope it will serve as a cheerful chart for your sailing and a map to paradise that I pray more of us will try to follow.

Setting Sail for Paradise:

How to Chart a Pleasurable Life

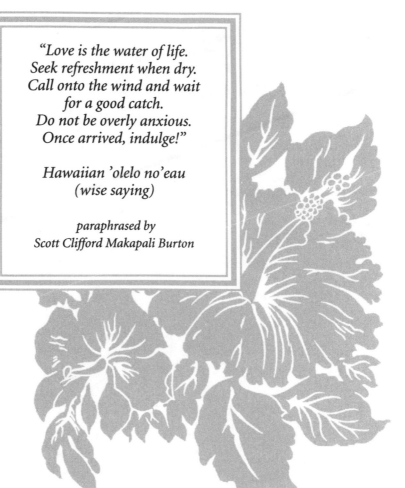

"Love is the water of life.
Seek refreshment when dry.
Call onto the wind and wait
for a good catch.
Do not be overly anxious.
Once arrived, indulge!"

Hawaiian 'olelo no'eau
(wise saying)

paraphrased by
Scott Clifford Makapali Burton

In This Section, You'll Learn

. . . the essential techniques of the pleasure navigator, including:

The Third Way—the Oceanic Way of pleasure

How to think like a navigator and step outside the stressful bounds of Western life

The SAFE technique for developing a happier "in-look" on life

How to avoid "near-life experiences" and become fully alive

How to live in the blissful *pono,* or balance, of life

How to use pleasure prompters for daily doses of delight

How to "catch your breath" and share life's sacred breath with others

How to test your pleasure quotient and learn about your psychoimmunity

The Five Cs of *aloha*

Welcomes and warnings for your journey into pleasure

Chapter One

Ten Ways of the Cheerful Navigator:
Learning to Change Our Minds

'Au i ke kai me he manu ala
Pronounced slowly, one syllable at a time,
as "ah-oo ee kay kah-ee may hey ma-new ah-la"

Cross the sea as a bird

If you're going to try to change your life for more pleasure, you first have to change your mind. You have to consider a Third Way to a happier, hardier life for yourself and everyone around you—the way of the sea, rather than the Eastern or Western orientations to daily life. The Oceanic Way is fundamentally different in its approach to living (see table below for more details).

Person, Place, or Thing?

Much of Western culture is grounded in "things" to be used by the individual, while Eastern culture is based more in "person," learning more about the self. The Polynesian Way is based mostly on "place." The Polynesians are people of the land and their idea of *aloha 'aina,* or love of the land, is central to the pleasure prescription. A Polynesian man told me, "We are at home. So many people who come here seem lost and emotionally or spiritually homeless. They keep moving, but they never really live anywhere. We love being in our place in the sea. We will never leave because we *are* this place."

Our land-locked minds have trouble comprehending the physical "place" of the island nations of Polynesia. If what we call the Polynesian Triangle were superimposed over the European continental mass, it would encompass an area stretching from London across Northern Europe to Siberia, down to China and Tibet, over to southwestern Asia, and back up to Southern Europe and England—a "Eurasian triangle" that includes the better part of two continents. It is the people in this Eurasian triangle who, though they think they have conquered and dominated the world with their strong personalities and abundant things, have really failed to claim their natural birthright of bliss through a profound sense of place.

To explain his concept of place, one Polynesian *kahuna* told me, "The world thinks that we are islands far off in the sea, but we do not see that. Continental people live in cities and countries separated by boundaries on the land. We are part of one big family all connected in the sea. We travel on water roads. We are small islands far from the larger islands Westerners call continents. Their continents are just larger islands in the sea, but they don't seem connected by anything. They are moving farther and farther away from each other. Perhaps their islands are just too big and they can't see beyond them to know that they are all connected. They think in terms of lines and borders, so maybe that's why they thought for so long that the Earth was flat. We have known for thousands of years that Earth itself is an island in the cosmic sea. We are all navigators, not owners. We are all on a canoe in the sky."

—from *The Pleasure Prescription*

To be a good pleasure-prescription writer means to *holoholo* (pronounced "ho-low ho-low"), to try for what one executive who now pauses for more pleasure describes as "a gleeful glide instead of a tough climb through life." Most of us have a Western brain that urges us to keep going, getting, accomplishing, and conquering. But to be a pleasure-prescription writer, you first have to start thinking like a navigator rather than a general—living in the sea of life rather than climbing mountains, overcoming obstacles, and defending territory.

Why do we need to change our mind, to consider this Third Way of living? If we don't, our health may suffer. Since our Western mind thinks more like a general trying to maintain control than like a sailor enjoying a cruise, we spend much of our time trying to master and fix our way to health rather than trying to maintain our natural state of joyful being. We see sickness and suffering as things that require repair, rather than signs of a need for natural balance and connection. As a result of this constant struggle, our Western brain has little time for the simple joys of life and ends up suffering from Delight Deficiency Syndrome (see the table on page 22). The Western brain is tormented by fear of failure, fear of early death, and the daily pressures of doing more and more; it is constantly trying to get what it wants, to be all it can be. If you are going to learn to write your own pleasure prescriptions, begin right now by trying to be less of a general in the daily wars of living, and more of a Polynesian navigator sailing happily through—not to—paradise.

Checking for Delight Deficiency Syndrome

How many of the symptoms below, each of which begins with the letter C, do you have?

1. *Chronic fatigue,* usually accompanied by difficulty sleeping or sleep onset insomnia (falling asleep immediately, waking in a few hours, and then not being able to get back to sleep).

2. *Constriction,* usually experienced as a stiffness in the "tense muscle triad" of the forehead, neck, and upper shoulders.

3. *Chronophobia,* fear of having too much to do in too little time.

4. *Consumerism,* a constant need to get more, better, newer stuff.

5. *Feeling conflicted,* torn between the need to be with your spouse, family, and friends and still fulfill work obligations.

6. *Feeling cornered,* trapped between daily obligations and dreams of a life not pursued.

7. *Being controlling,* feeling that you must stay on top of things or they will get ahead of you, or that others are trying to take advantage or control of you.

8. *Feeling challenged,* feeling that you must prove yourself constantly or someone else might "get your piece of the pie."

9. *Becoming careless,* making mistakes in even the simplest and most common activities.

10. *Being cynical,* expressed in sarcasm, being unwilling to trust people, and having difficulty enjoying what would seem to be enjoyable activities because they seem frivolous or distracting.

The more you find yourself suffering from these symptoms, the more likely you are suffering from Delight Deficiency Syndrome. Fortunately, there is a cure for this: daily doses of pleasure!

—from *The Pleasure Prescription*

To assess your own brain's bias toward a Western or an Oceanic way of thinking, see the table on page 24. Circle the words from either column that best describe your brain's orientation.

The more words you circled in the right-hand column, the more your brain thinks in the Oceanic Way and the easier it will be for you to write your own pleasure prescriptions.

Western	Oceanic
The general	The navigator
Objectivity	Subjectivity
Emotional distance	Total involvement
Avoid illness	Celebrate health
Nature is "out there"	We are part of nature
Mastery of nature	Responsibility for nature
Inner child	Inner elder
Techniques	Rituals
We have individual souls	We share a soul
Secular	Sacred
Written words, numbers	Chants, songs, myths
Competitive	Collaborative
Family is secondary to self-fulfillment	Family is focus of life
Body is a vehicle for brain	Body and mind are one
Self-excellence	Group excellence
Power	Unity
Sex	Sensuality
Ownership	Sharing
Smart	Wise
Clever	Pleasant

Below you'll find some key ideas to keep in your mind as you set sail for more pleasurable loving, working, playing, and healing.

Ten Ways of the Cheerful Navigator

1. *Think of yourself as a navigator sailing the seas of life, not as a general fighting for your life.* The cheerful navigator is a connector, not a com-

mander. Pause frequently during the day to envision yourself as a navigator sailing around the lush green islands of a Polynesian paradise, cruising on the deep blue ocean under the pure white clouds, and feeling the gentle, warm trade winds on your face.

2. *Want what you have, rather than trying to get what you want.* The cheerful navigator "sails to sail" and enjoys the rewards of simple destinations arrived at after a pleasant passage. She does not try hard to "get there" or, once arrived, try to conquer, possess, and protect territory. For the cheerful navigator, the voyage is its own reward. Take time every day to look around you to enjoy what you already have and remember that, no matter where you think you are going, you are going to have to live with yourself and the results of how you traveled once you get there.

3. *Instead of fighting or fleeing when your life becomes stressful, go with the flow.* The cheerful navigator says *"Mae e holo ana"* (pronounced "mah-ay ay ho-low ah-nah"), meaning "go with however it goes." Remember that pleasure cannot be pursued; it must ensue from being with life, rather than doing things in order to make your life happy. Try repeating the navigator's *"mae e holo ana,* mah-ay ay ho-low ah-nah" when you feel land-locked in stressful living.

4. *Try to have less rather than more.* Too much "stuff" can make your life very heavy, your canoe very difficult to sail, and take all the fun out of your journey. If you try to take too much stuff to paradise, you will never get there. Try once every month to get rid of some of your stuff.

5. *Try to do less.* Too much interference with the canoe's sailing can cause the canoe to swamp. The cheerful navigator joins with the canoe and lets it sail him. He watches, feels, senses, and listens for "the way" instead of trying to *get* his way. Every day, resolve that you will skip doing something or will try to do a little less.

6. *Say "no" rather than "yes" to opportunities.* The cheerful navigator is not tempted by shortcuts or illusions on the distant and ever-elusive horizon. She happily stays the course and realizes that there is nothing wrong with drifting once in a while and that the horizon ahead will always be ahead. It serves as a symbol of joyful traveling; it is not an ultimate objective. Once a day, don't just do something, sit there.

7. *Give up control.* The cheerful navigator is free to follow the wind, read the waves, listen to the birds, and sense what the fish are saying. She charts the course but is only the eyes of the canoe. She is a part of the crew, not in charge of it. Every day, let someone else take control. Go along, give in, and don't fight. Let the eager driver move ahead of you.

8. *Think less about winning.* The cheerful navigator doesn't care about being first to paradise. He realizes that he is already there and knows in his heart that the voyage itself is heaven on earth. As often as possible, play games without scoring or winners. When your life is full of contests, your rewards will be hollow victories that will only make you seek more victories.

9. *Think less about time.* The cheerful navigator is not in a race against time. She knows that time won't run out, and she also knows that running can cause us to race past life itself. She is in tune with the seasons, the stars, the sun, and the moon, not the clock. Think of seasons more than seconds, and moments more than months. One day a week, don't wear your watch.

10. *Think and do more, much more, about and with your family.* The cheerful navigator puts his family first in all things and extends the concern he feels for his family to strangers as well. For the cheerful navigator, everyone is crew on Canoe Earth. Once every day, pause at work or wherever you find yourself and spend a few minutes looking at family pictures.

Now take a pleasure pause and reflect on the Ten Ways. How might you begin applying them to your life? Write your answers below, one answer for each of the Ten Ways.

_____

_____

_____

_____

_____

If you are trying to think like a Polynesian navigator right now, you are ready to set sail for a wonderful, joyful, fun voyage. Your Western brain may not want you to go sailing, but your brain is not you. If your brain is telling you that you're silly, strange, abnormal, or unrealistic for trying to think in the Oceanic Way, just think of your brain as a frightened child. Patiently tell it that if it will relax, trust, and give up a little control, it will not get seasick and that it will learn to love sailing. Remember that your Western brain suffers from "divine-ophobia." It irrationally thinks that if it gives in and lets you acknowledge and awaken all of the glory, grandeur, and magnificence of just being alive, you will stop striving and start living in a gentle and quiet bliss that it finds frightening. Comfort your timid brain and let it know that it is sailing toward more healthy pleasure than it ever dreamed possible.

Now I'll describe another technique that you may find useful when you're trying to change your mind and quiet your brain.

Thirty-Minute Doses of Delight

Decide now that you are going to spend no more and no less than one half-hour every day with this book—I call these times "thirty-minute doses of delight." No matter how much you want to continue reading and working with this book, stop after one half-hour. No matter how much you want to stop before a half-hour or want to skip a day of working on your pleasure prescriptions, stay with this book for the full half-hour. If you miss a day, just go back to your thirty-minute delight doses the next day. If thirty minutes seems too little time, that's fine. You'll look forward to returning to the book. If thirty minutes every day seems impossible or if your brain is fighting the idea of taking thirty-minute delight doses, remember that part of your finding a more balanced and pleasurable daily life is making the commitment to your thirty minutes of "pleasure prescribing," whether your Western brain wants you to or not.

To help free your land-locked brain still more, sail on to Chapter Two to learn how to quiet your Western brain and free your indigenous Polynesian mind for a more blissful, joyful pleasure passage through life.

Chapter Two

Keeping Your Mind on Your Happiness: How to Have a Happier, More Balanced "In-Look"

Loa'a ke alo i halua a ola
Pronounced slowly, one syllable at a time, as
"low-ah ah kay ah-low ee ha-lew-ah ah oh-la"

Happiness in life is obtained in the house of life

For our prehistoric ancestors, life was a matter of "survival of the most pessimistic." Expecting the worst and watching out for predators and the countless threats of daily life helped them stay alive. Even though our modern world still has many threats, life today is nowhere near as dangerous as it was for our ancient forebears. To learn to write your own pleasure prescriptions, you have to overcome your evolutionary tendency to look for the worst in people and the world and start looking for the best.

Instead of always looking out for danger and crises, a pleasurable life is based on a rational, balanced looking in for that sense that seems to say, "This is really great." A happy in-look doesn't mean foolish and reckless denial of the bitter realities of life; instead, it means being more alert to the wonders, common miracles, and simple gifts of just being alive. In this chapter, I'll teach you a number of skills that can help you develop a happier, more balanced in-look: the SAFE and *no'ono'o nui* contemplation techniques; focusing and strengthening your *pono* (balance); and using "pleasure-prompter" questions to focus and relax your mind.

The SAFE Technique (Feeling Fascination)

Now that you have begun to "change your mind" and to think more like a cheerful Polynesian navigator who enjoys sailing in the canoe more than getting to the island, here is a way to develop a happy in-look by keeping your mind on your joy: the SAFE—Sit And Feel Every-thing—technique.

The SAFE technique, put simply, is the act of intensely doing nothing at all. In Western culture, hard work, action, productivity, and keeping busy are highly valued. But writing pleasure prescriptions is based on the Oceanic Way of being present in the world, so that the world can connect with you. The SAFE technique encourages this connection by providing a quiet time in which your seventh sense for pleasure (see the table below) can awaken and help you feel and drink in all that life offers.

The Seventh Sense

We live primarily by five basic senses: sight, smell, taste, touch, and hearing. Sometimes we experience a sixth, "psychic" sense, which conveys and reads an energy we cannot always describe or measure. Our six senses evolved to make sure that we seek what we need to survive and that we avoid things that threaten our survival. Beyond these physical and psychic senses, though, is a seventh sense, one that modern society often fails to nurture. It is an intuitiveness composed of all the basic senses. It directs and employs the other senses to detect what is true healthy pleasure. Consider it an evolutionary sense for bliss and an enchantment with living.

The seventh sense mediates all of the basic senses and gives them purpose. The seventh sense is the gestalt of all of our basic six senses and more than the sum of them. It is the "something tells me there is something missing, something more" sense. The seventh sense is subtle; it gets our attention by entering our consciousness and inspiring us to think about a meaningful, joyful, enjoyable life.

The seventh sense regulates the brain, mind, and body and ensures that we "feed" ourselves the basic things necessary for happiness and health. Like food for the body, the seventh sense seeks food for the soul. The seventh sense is a moderator; if we follow it, it will direct us away from what hurts us and lead us directly to what brings us and others the greatest joy and health. My study of the links between current medical research and Oceanic tradition has convinced me that the way of feeling, thinking, and behaving in the world that the Polynesians called *aloha* is the key to the discovery and development of your own seventh sense.

—from *The Pleasure Prescription*

The SAFE technique involves three steps. First, you have to stop physically and mentally moving. Once each day, sit down in a quiet place with as many living things around you as possible. Plants, pets, grass, trees, sand, water, and soil contain immense healing energy that we pass right by with our busy bodies. Next, stop doing and thinking and try just feeling. Quiet your busy brain by having no goals, expectations, or agenda. Just be. Listen for your heart, the song of a bird, the trickle of a small stream, or the wind in a backyard bush. Just sit and feel everything and anything. Don't be selective. If the phone rings, hear it and forget it. When you are SAFE, free yourself at least for a few moments to just be with the world.

There is a paradox in the SAFE technique. Most of us who practice it regularly notice that just doing nothing and feeling everything tend to produce powerful results. You will likely notice that your SAFE period is followed by receipt of good news, the resolution of a problem that you may have experienced, or the emergence of new life possibilities. Why this "good result from doing nothing" happens is not important. Just do what the Hawaiians do—hang loose!

When you use the SAFE technique, remember that it is not a meditation method but a "fascination" focus. It doesn't ask you to disconnect or tune out, but to become completely aware of your surroundings, the people around you, and even people and places of times past—truly and wholly sensing the interconnectedness of the world. It is a way to be a child again and to allow yourself to be re-enchanted by the simple things of life, to feel the sacred breath of life in every cell of your body, and to feel energized by the subtle energy that is all around you, flowing within and from everyone and everything.

No'ono'o Nui

At the end of this chapter, I'm going to ask you three questions important to your pleasure-prescription writing. Your responses to these questions will predict to large measure how long, how happily, and how well you and those around you will live. To be able to most accurately answer these questions, you have to be willing to do something that has helped the Polynesians achieve remarkable, healthy balance in their lives and the lives of their families. You have to learn to *no'ono'o nui* (pronounced "no oh-no-oh new-ee")—meaning "to peacefully and contemplatively connect with the experience of being alive." This is an essential part of forming your *aloha* alliance (as described in this book's introduction) and properly using pleasure prescriptions.

It doesn't matter if you sit alone or with those you care about when you *no'ono'o nui*. This is not an individual meditation technique. It is a way to reawaken to the joy of the energy of life flowing within and among all persons and things—the way Polynesians stay fascinated with life.

To *no'ono'o nui*, think during your SAFE time about those you love and have loved. Think about some wonderful time you shared with someone else. Feel your body. Look for the beauty around you, but don't compare and contrast it with anything else. A lovely, blooming tree is gorgeous, but a long-dead tree creates a mysterious pattern against the sky and provides lines for your creation of wondrous images. A deep green lawn is pretty to look at, but burned grass in shades of yellow, orange, and light green, varied with spots of brown soil, tells a story about the experience of that part of the earth. Don't judge, absorb. Remember that *no'ono'o nui* is a process of connection, not isolation. It is a process of reminding your brain that you are in charge and reawakening to the fact that your gift of life is in your own hands and is yours to waste or celebrate. (See the table below for another *no'ono'o nui* idea.)

A Chant to Reawaken *(Ho'ala Hou)*

Don't let your SAFE time become an obligation. Use this book to have fun learning new ways to release the natural pleasure psychochemicals that are waiting to flow within you. Slow yourself down and reawaken your indigenous brain by resisting your Western brain's panicked insistence that you don't have enough time to SAFE or that you are wasting its time. To assist you in slowing down—what a Polynesian navigator would call *ho'olohi* (meaning "take it easy" and pronounced "ho-oh low-ee")—you may want to use another Polynesian technique I introduced earlier: gentle chanting.

During your SAFE time, *no'ono'o nui* (calmly reflect) by speaking aloud the Hawaiian phrase *"ho'ala hou"*—pronounced "ho ah-lah ho-oo" and meaning "to reawaken," to become alert again to what we already know deep inside our soul.

I am president and CEO of a research corporation called Ho'ala Hou. Its mission is to learn, research, and apply the ancient lessons of Polynesia to modern life and to attempt to connect the best of modern science and medicine with the some of the world's oldest and wisest ideas about living. Much of this joy book is based on what Ho'ala Hou has learned. Ho'ala Hou's

research indicates that by just slowly and gently pronouncing each syllable in Polynesian phrases like
"ho'ala hou," you can begin to find more joyful balance
in your immune system and in your working, loving,
playing, and healing.

When practicing this chant, don't be afraid to sound
funny, don't yield to your brain's impatience with such
a gentle set of sounds, and don't be afraid to be a little
"abnormal."

Avoiding Near-Life Experiences

If you don't take time to *no'ono'o nui* and if you don't make SAFE time
every day, you may end up at risk for near-life experiences. As one
kahuna explains it, "If you don't *no'ono'o nui* every day, you die before
you are ever born. You may have only near-life experiences and never
really, fully feel what it is to be alive. You will be so busy trying to do the
best *hula* that you will forget to listen for the lessons of the *mele* [song
or chant] that is the rhythm of life. You can't *hula* with health and joy if
you listen only to the sounds of 'now.' You must relax and tune in to all
the sounds that ever were and the songs being sung to you by your ancestors."

To *no'ono'o nui* and do the SAFE technique, make a commitment
that you will take the time once a day to sit down quietly, try to shut out
distractions by using your *ho'ala hou* chant (see the exercise), stop trying to win the human race, and listen for all the songs and breathe all of
the breaths that have ever been. Don't die with all of your songs left un-
sung and all of the songs of life left unheard.

Pono: Blissful Balance

Learning balance is also an essential part of developing your happier in-
look. Much of our modern life is led out of balance or without what
Hawaiians call *pono.* Our "busy body" is so constantly urged on by our

stimulation-addicted brain that we seem to be always getting ready to go, or going, but never really feeling that we are "there." We become disconnected from the *'aina,* those around us, and the comforting wisdom of those who came before us. We end up feeling that, despite our many timesaving devices, we have failed to save enough time to do what we feel we really want to do.

To Hawaiians, the word *pono* means much more than just "balance." It also means "good," "correct," "righteous," "virtuous," "fair," and "the way things not only are, but have always been meant to be." *Pono* is living "the way," not getting "our" way. (The closest English word I have found to *pono* is *copacetic,* meaning that everything is the way it is supposed to be.) Its implied sense of righteousness is not a legalistic or judgmental righteousness, but a spiritual balance that derives from connection and caring. To live in *pono* is to connect with everyone and everything. Only when everyone and everything around you is safe and well can you be in *pono,* because you are a part of the world.

I'll remind you several times, throughout the course of this book, to consider *pono* in relation to your own life. I'll do so to remind your brain that there is another way to think about living. When you feel stressed, land-locked into the human race, or feel that learning to write pleasure prescriptions is just too difficult, remember that these feelings are merely your Western brain's attempts to distract you from your journey to paradise. When your brain is screaming at you to stop your pleasure-prescription program, take a pleasure pause for a few moments and say the word *pono.* Remember to re-enchant your way through the rough times in your pleasure-prescription program.

At the same time, realize that perfect balance is not something you can achieve. You cannot achieve complete "self"-balance, because you are in this life with everyone and everything. Nothing in life is static, nothing—including you—is isolated, and nothing about this life is under your complete control. Like a paddler in a canoe, you are affected by the sea and other paddlers, and you affect them as well. We have to be alert to our personal balance, but we will overturn the canoe if we try too hard to establish perfect balance, ignore the other paddlers' balance, or go through life in constant fear of capsizing. Just as none of us is ever in total health but always in transitional and varying states of well-being (from very sick to very healthy), all of life is in a dynamic state. You are never "in balance," but great joy comes from the process of balancing. The fun of life is in the act of balancing, not in obtaining final and total equilibrium.

Pleasurable balance is ultimately a series of shifts—a little to the left, a little to the right, a little up on the wave, and then a little down. As the Hawaiian disk jockey Boy Kanahe once said, "When things don't go right, take 'em to the left." *Pono* is the feeling that we are experiencing healthy joy despite the pressures and challenges of the trip, a joy made possible by our *aloha* alliance with the world, a joy that comes from our interconnected and ever-changing balance.

You might now think back to the question asked at the start of this book: "Would those who know me best say that I am a total pleasure to live, love, play, and work with?" Take a pleasure pause and consider this question in terms of balance. Did you answer that you may be a pleasure to be with at work but that you're often a menace to family peace and joy at home? Did you answer that you are a real pleasure at home but an aggravation to others at work? Did you answer that you are a pleasure to work, live, and love with but, when it comes to play—golf, cards, tennis, or other activities—you can be a real party pooper because of your competitive nature? Did you answer that you seem to be a pleasure to others but a real pain to yourself? Then you need to remember that pleasure is *pono*. Healthy pleasure not only requires a determined, insistent attempt to stay connected with others and the world, but it also demands the extension of that joyful connection to all areas of daily living. We cannot focus on just one aspect of living—be it work, family relationships, or sports. We need to focus on our lives in their entirety, seeking balance everywhere.

Hula for Happiness

To obtain maximum pleasure from this book, you not only have to speak up. You also have to get up. *Makaukau?* (Ready?—pronounced "mah-kah-oo-kah-oo.") It's time to *hula!*

Hula is a body prayer, a way of tuning in, connecting with, and moving in resonance with the energy of the land and the ever-present energy of the ancestors. When one does the *hula* with complete respect for its sacred meaning, one feels the presence of all those who came before us. One feels the past and future in one's heart. *Hula* is a process of sacred connection with ancestors, the earth, and the breath of life.

Hula is also the perfect example of healthy balance. Echoing the in-and-out rhythm of breath, a *hula* dancer gently moves left and right, back and forth, and up and down in complete connection with the rhythm of life.

The most basic of *hula* steps is called *kaholo* (pronounced "ka-ho-low"). It is done by extending one foot to the side and bringing the other foot alongside the first. Then the same is done on the other side. The shoulders are kept straight, the knees are bent slightly, and the arms and hands are held chest-high and moved gently side to side, like surf ebbing to and fro.

Hula for your own health by standing up, smiling, breathing deeply, and doing the *kaholo*. This step, like all of *hula*, must only be done with respect. *Hula* is a means of "entrainment," or getting in complete balance and connection, not just "entertainment." It is a very powerful way of connecting and balancing your life, but only if it is done with the same sense of reverence for the *'aina* and *na kupuna* from which *hula* was born and which still nurture the dance today.

Three Pleasure-Prompter Questions

Working toward balance and developing a happier in-look, of course, are not easy tasks. Your brain, trapped in a land-locked Western orientation, sometimes requires a little prompting. The three pleasure-prompter questions presented in this section can help get your attention and help you focus on thinking less like a stressed cosmopolitan warrior and more like a joyful, wise Polynesian.

During one of your SAFE times, *no'ono'o nui* by writing your answers to the following three questions in the Before space provided below. Leave the After space for writing in after you have finished reading this joy book.

While you're considering your answers, remember to slow down and connect completely with these questions. As suggested earlier, don't just read, verbalize! Read each of the following questions and all of the assignments in this book out loud, write your answers, and then read your answers out loud. If you have a tape recorder, you may want to tape your responses. You can listen to your answers in your car, if you feel rushed or feel that you must do more than one thing at a time. You can also sit with someone else (have that person use their own copy of this book), listen to your answers together, and discuss their meaning to you, your relationships, and the unmet pleasure potential in your daily loving, working, and playing.

1. Are you smiling right now? Are you taking great pleasure at this moment in being alive, seeing, thinking, and feeling?

Answer yes or no here: _____

Now write down how you are feeling and looking at this moment. Describe the look on your face, your body posture, how you think you might look to others around you, and how joyful you feel at this moment.

Before: _____

_____

_____

After: _____

_____

_____

2. Do you regularly make others smile? Do you bring great pleasure every day to both your family and strangers? Do people love to be around you, look forward to seeing you, and speak well about you? (Another way of phrasing this question is to ask if you would want to be around yourself all of the time.)

Answer yes or no here: _____

Describe the time and place you last shared meaningful pleasure with someone, and describe the person with whom you shared it.

Before: _____

_____

_____

_____

_____

After: _____

_____

_____

_____

_____

_____

3. Is Earth smiling because you are living with her? Is the fact that you are alive a source of great health, healing, and hardiness to the planet?

Answer yes or no here: _____

Describe the last time you did something that improved or protected the beauty and health of the planet, such as helping to protect the environment or helping an animal.

Before: _____

_____

_____

_____

_____

_____

After: _____

_____

_____

_____

_____

Remember to return to read the answers you wrote in the Before space after you complete this joy book and use the sixty prescriptions provided in it. Then, in the After space provided, write your new answers.

From the time we develop in the uterus, the sounds of our mother's voice and heartbeat resonate within us. A happy in-look is our birthright, but most of us, sadly, lose this gift by the time we've grown up. Rediscovering our happy in-look means tuning into and spiritually retrieving the sensations of our early days, the sights, smells, feelings, and tastes that became the most joyful memories of our life. It means being open, in our current lives, to those things and people that bring us joy. It means reaching for the balance and connection that bring true pleasure. Ultimately, developing a happy in-look is the ultimate attempt to connect deeply and profoundly with what it means to be alive on Planet Earth.

The Sounds of Paradise

Hawaiian music played by those who honor the culture of Hawai'i will help you in your simple but sacred *kaholo*. You can move with the gentle rhythms of Hawai'i and do *kaholo* or you can use this music during your pleasure pauses and SAFE times.

I suggest CDs by Frank Kawaikapuokalani Hewett, one of the most wise teachers of *hula* and most graceful of dancers in the Islands. His album *E Ho'omau Ka Ha O Ka Hawai'i* (Honor the Culture of Hawai'i) is perfect for your practice of Polynesian balance, and its songs teach many lessons about the healthy pleasures of *aloha,*

Another *kumu hula* (teacher of *hula*) is my Maui neighbor Keali'i Reichel. He too is a most wise, giving, and gentle *kumu hula,* and his compositions are lessons in life and love. His CDs are *Kawaipunahele* (The Sacred Place) and *Lei Hali'a* (A Lei of Fond Recollection).

Music by the Makaha Sons from the island of Ni'ihau is also beautifully infused with the *mana* of *aloha,* particularly their album *Ke Alaula* (The Dawning). The music of Israel Kamakawiwo'ole is both healing and joyful, particularly his album *E Ala E,* a celebration of the gentle dignity of the people of Hawai'i. My dear friends Keala Hussey and Lani Anduha, members of the group Hawaiian Heart, have a CD called *Te Tiare* (named after a Polynesian flower) that displays their lovely voices and the magic of Polynesia. Teresa Bright, Del Beazley, and other gifted artists have made many beautiful albums of Hawaiian music, and these too will bring much pleasure to your home.

The above CDs and the music of many other Hawaiian artists are available at Hawai'i Calls, Inc., 2290 Alahao Place, Honolulu, HI 96819-2283, (808) 847-4608, fax (808) 847-4609. They are also available on the island of Maui at Tropical Disc, Dolphin Plaza, 2395 South Kihei Road, Kihei, Maui, HI 96753, (808) 874-3000, fax (808) 879-5863, e-mail tropdisc@naui .net. If you order, please be sure to tell the salesperson that Dr. Pearsall sends his *mahalo* (thanks) and *aloha* to his neighbors, whose music helped save his life.

Chapter Three

Are You Breathless or Blissful?
How to Catch Your Breath

Mauli ola
Pronounced "mah-oo-lee oh-lah"

"The breath of life," meaning a toast to tenderness and an
invitation to connect with the sacredness of life

We are all given the sacred breath of life. Unfortunately, we often lead
breathless lives or feel "out of breath," *pauaho* in Hawaiian. We are so
driven in our daily work that our body desperately demands air to
breathe. Sometimes we even "stress sigh" in an involuntary expiration,
saying "ahh" as we exhale. Involuntary "ahh-ing" is a sure sign that you
are leading a breathless life.

To learn to write your own pleasure prescriptions, you must slow
down, sit down, and catch your breath back from wherever your
stressed living has been sending it. As you read these words, are you
breathing slowly, deeply, and fully? If not, and if your Western brain is
bothering you with its thoughts of getting up, getting going, and doing
something else, put this manual down, sit back, smile, and take some
deep breaths. Try saying "ahh" as you exhale. Conscious stress sighs,
used for relaxation, are a great prescription for pleasure.

Are You *Haole* (Leading a Breathless Life)?

The Polynesian word *haole* means to be without *(ole)* breath *(ha)*. It was originally applied to missionaries who prayed so quickly that the Polynesians thought they must have no breath. One major stress sign and a symptom of a joyless life is a failure to breathe deeply and abdominally. We become so rushed by our selfish brain that we begin to breathe just enough to keep our brain alive but not enough to nourish our soul. We become chest breathers, taking in tiny doses of life-giving air but not using our abdomen or breathing deeply and fully enough to nourish our heart with abundant oxygen. We begin to deprive our heart of the oxygen it needs, and thus we set the stage for cardiovascular disease or heart attacks.

Try your own "breath test." Sit down, place your hand on your lower abdomen, watch your hand, and breathe in as deeply as you can. Your hand should move outward. If your hand does not move, you are breathing with your chest. Take several pleasure pauses during the day, put on your Hawaiian music (see Chapter Two for some recommendations), and practice deep abdominal breathing with the music. Record what you observe during these pleasure pauses in the space below.

_____

_____

_____

_____

_____

_____

_____

_____

_____

_____

Remember, we breathe as we think and we think as we breathe. If we are patient, harmonious, agreeable, humble, and kind, we breathe deeply and fully. If we are impatient, disconnected, hostile, selfish, and rough, we breathe in a shallow, rapid way, the style designed for fighting and fleeing, not flowing.

To best write and fill your own pleasure prescriptions, you have to catch your breath. Start to think of your life as taking place on an infinite ocean with storms, squalls, quiet times, beauty, harshness, and limitless routes to the same location, to be reached by an enjoyable cruise rather than a quick drive. Remember that there are no barriers on the ocean and that all boundaries are the illusions of a Western, landlocked mind—the general's mind—that tends to see the world in terms of territory to protect, space to own, and obstacles to overcome. For the Oceanic mind, riding out a storm instead of cursing it, sailing on the sea instead of trying to master or plunge through it, and working as a member of a crew rather than always trying to be a captain is the healthy way to live.

Aloha: To Share the Sacred Breath

In Hawaiian, one of the meanings of *aloha* is "to share the sacred breath" (*alo*, "to share," and *ha*, "breath"). When you take your SAFE time and your thirty-minute doses of delight, here's another *no'ono'o nui*, or connective and contemplative exercise, that you can do that should make your pleasure-prescription writing easier.

You have learned to chant the words *ho'ala hou* as a technique to get your busy brain's attention. Another *no'ono'o nui* technique is repeating the word *aloha* to yourself. Take a deep breath in through your nostrils and say *"alo"* to yourself silently. (Remember, as you breathe in, that *alo* means "to share.") Next, breathe slowly out through your mouth and softly say *"ha"* aloud. Repeat, saying *"alo"* to yourself as you breathe in and softly saying *"ha"* aloud as you exhale.

Try this *aloha* breathing exercise five times, one time for each of the five elements of *aloha* (patience, unity, agreeableness, humbleness, and kindness). Think of each of the five *aloha* elements each time you breathe out and say the word *"ha."* Think "patience" as you say *"ha,"* then on your next exhalation think "unity," and so on. This *aloha no'ono'o nui* will feel awkward at first, but after some practice, it will become almost automatic, and doing this *no'ono'o nui* will eventually teach your brain to think in terms of an *aloha* rather than a *haole* life. You will find that your busy body becomes less busy and that your brain will shut up for a while, letting you feel relaxed enough to enjoy being alive.

Chapter Four

Stocking Up for a Joyful Life Cruise:
The Five Cs of Pleasure

"God created man. He breathed into his nostrils the breath
of life, and man became a living soul."
GENESIS 2:7

In *The Pleasure Prescription* and in this companion to that book, I've
described in detail the ancient and sacred Oceanic concept of *aloha*. As
you take the sixty pleasure prescriptions in Section Three of this book,
you will combine the five components of *aloha* into a pleasure potion
that allows you to catch your breath and to "con-spire" (to breathe together with others) in a more joyful, blissful, balanced life.

The five components of *aloha* are patience, unity, agreeableness,
humbleness, and kindness. These elements continue to be verified as
lifesavers by modern research in the fields of psychoneuroimmunology
(PNI) and psychoneurocardiology (PNC). Both of these fields study
the interaction of the mind, heart, body, and soul with other people, the
planet, and the cosmos. The pleasure prescriptions you are learning to
take and write are based on a combination of the Third Way—the
Oceanic Way—and the best and newest information about well-being,
healing, and happiness that Western medicine has to offer.

As you begin your lessons in pleasure-prescription writing, remember that each of the prescriptions you will write must contain five ingredients of the magic elixir of healthy pleasure. Be sure to check each
of your prescriptions for the proper, even balance of these components.

When a Polynesian navigator takes on supplies for the journey, he carefully counts and recounts to be sure that the most basic necessities are on board. Too much baggage and the voyage can become a struggle to transport and protect rather than explore and enjoy. Too little baggage and he may find himself without food or supplies.

In that spirit, here is your basic pleasure cruise supply list. Check each item carefully, because you will need every bit of these crucial stores, particularly at those times when the going gets rough. And remember—in contrast to the Western warning that "when the going gets tough, the tough get going," Polynesian pleasure is based on the idea that "when the going gets tough, sometimes it's a sign that you should stop going." This supply list extends the five components of *aloha* I presented in *The Pleasure Prescription* by adding the Five Cs of Pleasure.

The Five Cs of Pleasure

The five letters of the word *aloha* serve as the basic formula for concocting any pleasure prescription. Once you have the basic formula in place, the task is to fashion your pleasure prescription to fit your own needs in love, work, play, and healing.

So far in this joy book, you have tried to start thinking like a navigator, chosen to take some SAFE time to *no'ono'o nui* (reflect on the joy of living), and asked yourself the "three pleasure-prompter questions." As you re-stock to continue your trip, check out your *aloha* status.

A: Ahonui: Patience, Expressed with Perseverance
Pleasure Rx Concoction: C for Calmness

As you read through this book and learn about pleasure prescriptions, remember to take time to SAFE (sit and feel everything) in a quiet, tranquil, peaceful place. Such a place is not easy to find in our hurried, hectic, noisy world, but we all need a place to pause for pleasure. If you can, set up your own pleasure place in your home and return to it every time you read in this book. Your pleasure place doesn't have to be anything complicated; just find a corner where you can get what most of us want—a little peace and quiet. Let your family know that this will now be your pleasure place.

Some suggestions for a good pleasure place:

1. Outdoors if possible. If not, a place with some plants or animals and natural sounds—perhaps recordings of wave sounds or wind.

2. A place without distractions. Avoid televisions, phones, answering machines, and computers.

3. A place with pictures of family, favorite places, and pets.

4. A place as free as possible from the humming noises of air conditioners, radios, and televisions.

5. A place where you can be very comfortable without getting sleepy.

6. A place where you have some good memories of past experiences—such as the corner in your house where you put up the Christmas tree each year or celebrate other religious rituals.

L: Lokahi: Unity, Expressed Harmoniously
Pleasure Rx Concoction: C for Collaboration

Pleasure prescriptions, like the sacred breath, are made to be shared. You may make your entries in this book and read it in your private pleasure place, but the results of your efforts should be shared with as many people as possible.

As I pointed out earlier, another important part of learning to write pleasure prescriptions is finding a pleasure-prescription partner. Find someone who wants to put more pleasure into her or his life and the world in general. This person can be a friend, your spouse, a relative, even a co-worker. Agree to learn and experience the lessons of pleasure prescriptions together.

O: 'Olu'olu: Agreeableness, Expressed with Pleasantness
Pleasure Rx Concoction: C for Consideration

Approach learning to write and use pleasure prescriptions with an open heart and mind toward others. You may experience the temptation to blame others for your lack of pleasure or for making it difficult for you to lead a life of balanced joy. At such times, remember the "chain of consideration" rule of the pleasure prescription:

1. No matter what someone does or says to me, I always have a choice.

2. I can choose to try to change other people or to change how I think about other people.

3. It's very difficult to change other people.

4. I'll have to change how I think about other people.

5. How I think about other people can make my life a heaven or a hell on earth.

6. If I choose to make my own and other peoples' lives heaven on earth, I can do so by thinking more tolerantly, less impatiently, and more lovingly and forgivingly about other people.

Here's an example. If a driver cuts in front of you and then flashes you a vulgar sign, remember that you have a choice. You can choose to chase that person, flash a sign back, and do to your health what the vulgar sign suggests, or you can elect to think about that person differently. You can think, "That person is in a real hurry. He or she must be under pressure. Probably they're not usually impatient and rude. I know I get like that sometimes. They probably have their kinder times, too."

Remember that you are "response-able" and can choose your response to people and situations. Pleasure and pain are mainly in the brain! It's your choice.

H: Ha'aha'a: Humbleness, Expressed with Modesty
Pleasure Rx Concoction: C for Connection

Remember that unhealthy success is *pursued* and healthy success *ensues*. It ensues from the awareness that all of us are connected, whether we like it or not. None of us is better than another; the more separate we make ourselves, the sicker we get. The richer one's social networks, the lower the incidence of illness and death. By realizing that status is just an illusion that ultimately decreases pleasure, that different jobs, financial positions, and lifestyles are only illusory boundaries between us, and that two leading killers of our time are self-involvement and narrow self-concept, we help maintain the humble balance of who we really are and who we are not.

Writing pleasure prescriptions requires much less self-focus and more "other"-focus, along with a tolerant, generalized view of self-worth that is not dependent on any isolated aspect or part of life.

A: Akahai: Kindness, Expressed with Tenderness
Pleasure Rx Concoction: C for Compassion

One definition of the word "passion" is "to suffer." "Com-passion," then, means "to share suffering" or to "suffer together." As D.H. Lawrence wrote in *We Are Transmitters*, " 'Give, and it shall be given unto you' is still the truth about life." Your immune system is literally strengthened by compassionate caring and giving, and every pain of life is reduced by the power of kind benevolence. As you write your pleasure prescriptions, remember to check them for how much pleasure they will bring to others and how much suffering they will reduce.

Chapter Five

Know Your Starting Point:
Measuring Your Pleasure Quotient
and Psychoimmunity

He 'olina leo ka ke aloha
Pronounced "hey oh-lean-ah lay-oh ka kay ah-lo-ha"

A joyousness is in the voice of love

Our seventh sense responds to those people, things, and events that can bring us healthy, balanced pleasure in our daily living. It is the sense that taps into and releases the powerful endorphins and other pleasure psychochemicals that are our innate reward-for-living system. Beyond our six senses of sight, hearing, smell, taste, touch, and psychic perception, we have a profoundly subtle but extremely powerful sense for what brings our mind, heart, and soul healthy pleasure.

To assess the extent to which your seventh sense is functioning right now, it is helpful to know two things. First, what is your PQ—your pleasure quotient—at this time in your life? Secondly, what is your PI or psychoimmunity—how strong is the immune system that protects you from disease? This chapter helps you assess the degree to which your life is delightful, delighting, and healthful.

The Pleasure Prescription presented the *Aloha* Test. This joy book presents two new tests of *aloha* that help you understand how *aloha* can make your life happier and healthier by re-stimulating your seventh sense for pleasure. Before you embark on your journey into pleasure, assess your current pleasure quotient—the degree to which you are a pleased and pleasing person who extends *aloha* to everyone and everything—and your psychoimmunity—the degree to which your *aloha* levels are helping or hurting your health. Just as a doctor must determine the condition of her patient before prescribing any medication, it is helpful to assess your pleasure quotient and psychoimmunity as you prepare to write your own pleasure prescriptions.

WHAT'S YOUR PQ?
THE PLEASURE QUOTIENT TEST

SCORING

0 = Almost Never

1 = Sometines

2 = Often

3 = Very Often

4 = Almost Always

_____ People say I have a very nice smile.

_____ Other people smile at me.

_____ When I laugh, I laugh very hard.

_____ I take time to reflect on the good times in my life.

_____ I avoid conflicts and confrontations.

_____ I avoid ruminating about re-living, or going over and over angry encounters from the past.

_____ I am a lot of fun to be around.

_____ People tend to gather around me at social events.

_____ I take time to talk about things other than work with persons who call me about work-related issues.

_____ I "let things go easily" and do not hold grudges.

_____ I avoid saying negative things about people.

_____ I have a "thick skin," so criticism from others doesn't bother me.

_____ When I go to bed at night, I think very good thoughts about my life.

_____ I laugh easily.

_____ I cry easily.

_____ I feel like it would be great being married to me.

_____ I participate in things such as sing-alongs, dancing, games, and audience-involvement events.

_____ When I get sick, I get well very quickly.

_____ When I'm sick, I stop working and take time to just stay home and enjoy being sick and getting well.

_____ When I have complete privacy, I act silly, dance, and sing.

_____ I am moved to tears by beauty.

_____ I pray.

_____ I do not compare my happiness to that of others.

_____ I don't mind losing and appreciate when others win.

_____ I feel like I have and give off "good vibes."

TOTAL PLEASURE QUOTIENT SCORE _____

Interpreting Your PQ Score

The higher your PQ score, the more _aloha_ you already have as you learn to write your own pleasure prescriptions. Based on the research of Ho'ala Hou and the test results of hundreds of Hawaiians and Westerners, here is a scale to help you assess your PQ score.

The PQ Scale

90–100: Strong *aloha*
You are living with a very high degree of *pono* and should be a master pleasure-prescription writer and able to help others write their pleasure prescriptions.

70–89: Marginal *aloha*
You are living in a fairly good state of *pono,* but you will have to concentrate and avoid the distractions of your Western mind as you write your pleasure prescriptions.

60–69: *Aloha* deficit
You are leading your life out of *pono.* Be patient with yourself as you learn to write your pleasure prescriptions. It's going to take good effort and a lot of time, but the rewards will be very noticeable to you and those around you.

59 or below: *Aloha* depletion
You are far from a life of *pono.* You need immediate *kokua* (help) from a close friend or family member to begin the process of pleasure-prescription writing. It is likely that your spouse or close friend already knows you need *kokua,* so reach out now! You will not be able to learn to write your own pleasure prescriptions unless you talk about your efforts with another person. Take your time, stay with it, and don't let the brain that caused your score to be so low run and ruin your life.

Your PQ is not a fixed score, of course. None of us lives our life in constant *pono* and complete and fixed *aloha.* Take the Pleasure Quotient Test several times over the next few months. Discuss the results with your family and friends. Here are some suggestions for using the Pleasure Quotient Test to help you write your pleasure prescriptions:

▼ Pick one day every two or three weeks to regularly take the Pleasure Quotient Test. Record your scores—and the dates on which you took the test—below.

▼ Look for patterns in your scores. Does your score seem to go up or down in response to certain situations? What is it about those situations that influences your score?

▼ Each of the items on the Pleasure Quotient Test is a pleasure prescription in itself. Pick those items on which you scored poorly and try to change your behavior in that area.

▼ Have those who know you well score you. Ask them what they think about your score and what they think you could do to live a life of more *aloha*.

▼ Have someone at work score you. Take some staff *aloha* breaks and have everyone score themselves or each other and talk about their scores and how they might improve them.

The Pleasure Quotient Test is only a guide. You should not use it to make yourself feel guilty or to soothe yourself into complacency. Writing pleasure prescriptions is a lifelong process and each prescription will have a limited shelf life. As your life changes, so will your PQ score, your *aloha*, and the degree of *pono* in your life. Use the test much as a navigator observes the wind and waves to stay on course.

As you move on to the next test, remember that it is never too late to learn to write your own pleasure prescriptions. No matter how low your score, your innate pleasure system is just waiting to come alive within you.

Measuring Your Psychoimmunity

One of the most surprising results of the research of Ho'ala Hou was the discovery of the powerful relationship between Polynesian-style *aloha* pleasure and the status of an individual's and family's health, healing, and immunity. The test included in this section was used in our study.

In brief, Ho'ala Hou discovered that we do not "have" an immune system—we *are* our immune system. In addition, we are so connected with the *'aina* (Planet Earth) that we can actually become an "antigen" or aggravation to the earth's immune system. If we are not careful and do not start leading more pleasurable, patient, harmonious, agreeable, humble, kind lives, the earth's immune system is going to reject us. Our reckless disregard for our profound connection and interdependence with the planet has already resulted in attacks by deadly viruses that seek out human victims much as the antibodies of our immune system seek out antigens and foreign substances. Severe flooding due to overdevelopment and misuse of the land has cost many lives and washed away the dreams of thousands of families. The effects of global warming can seen from the windows of the space shuttle. As we worry so much about private ego, the earth upon which we all depend is suffering from our abuse. Writing eco-sensitive pleasure prescriptions that focus on bringing pleasure to the earth is the most important challenge we face in our modern world.

Pioneering researcher Dr. George Solomon is one of the founders of the field of psychoneuroimmunology (PNI). This is the field that is verifying that the 2,000-year-old Polynesian principles of *aloha* result in the healthy pleasure that keeps us well and heals us when we are sick. Ho'ala Hou drew on his research, the work of Henry Dreher (another astute student in the field of PNI), and the work of other PNI research leaders to produce this psychoimmunity test to let you know how urgently you need to start writing your own pleasure prescriptions. Chart your score, or just record it on the lines below.

WHAT'S YOUR PI?
THE PSYCHOIMMUNITY TEST

SCORING

0 = Almost Never

1 = Sometines

2 = Often

3 = Very Often

4 = Almost Always

_____ I have a sense of meaning and purpose in my daily work.

_____ I have a sense of safety, caring, and fulfillment in my family.

_____ My most intimate relationship is a source of great comfort and joy.

_____ I can let my anger be known without feeling really aggressive.

_____ I can ask for help and support whenever I need it.

_____ I get the support I need when I ask for it.

_____ I can say "no" when people ask favors if I don't really feel like doing them.

_____ I eat a diet that I think is good for me, and I do not feel guilty about not complying with someone else's ideas of "healthy eating."

_____ My form of exercise is fun and my own choice, not someone else's program.

_____ I play and can act foolish and childish.

_____ When I get depressed, I know I will bounce back.

_____ I'm an optimist.

_____ I confide everything about myself to someone.

_____ I'm very aware of my body and can read the signals it sends me about my health.

_____ I know my physical limits and do not exceed them.

_____ I know my emotional weak points and avoid aggravating them.

_____ I have a strong sense of control over my life.

_____ I have control over my time.

_____ I volunteer my time and give openly to strangers.

_____ I avoid putting all my eggs in one emotional basket and have many valued facets to my life.

_____ I enjoy it when other people make the decisions and have the power and control.

_____ I am relaxed when I drive and do not lose my temper.

_____ I receive a lot of sensuous and intimate body contact.

_____ I have a pet and really care about it.

_____ I do not take things personally.

    TOTAL PSYCHOIMMUNITY TEST SCORE _____

Interpreting Your PI Score

The higher your PI score, the more balanced your immune system probably is, the less likely you are to get sick, and the more likely you are to heal if you do become ill. Here is a scale to help you understand your PI status. It is based on Ho'ala Hou's research around the world. As is true of the Pleasure Quotient Test, hundreds of Polynesians took this test, along with hundreds of Westerners.

The PI Scale

90–100: Balanced psychoimmunity
You have a strong healing potential, which writing and using pleasure

prescriptions should help you strengthen and solidify. (The average Hawaiian's score on the Psychoimmunity Test was 91.)

80–89: Somewhat shaky psychoimmunity
You are vulnerable to small infections and the chronic, annoying symptoms of the minor diseases of civilization.

70–79: Shaky psychoimmunity
You are vulnerable to more serious, longer lasting, and more life-disruptive illnesses.

69 or below: Very shaky psychoimmunity
You are in dire need of more healthy, balanced, shared pleasure in your life. You are often an "antigen" to those around you and may be a challenge to their psychoimmunities.

Research into PNI is just beginning to learn about how the brain, body, immune system, and the world interact. Its preliminary findings have generated many more questions than answers. Simplistic, mind-over-body approaches to healing and assigning personal blame for illnesses are examples of the misuse of this young science and its often conflicting findings. What is clear, however, is that how we relate with others, how we feel about our life and its meaning, how we love, and how we work and play do influence our health. If you can say that your life is a pleasure and that the fact that you are alive is a pleasure for others and the world, PNI research strongly suggests that you have a leg up when it comes to well-being.

However, no matter what you've scored on the Psychoimmunity Test, take heart. You can start right now to improve your scores and improve your life. Pick one day every two or three weeks to regularly take the Psychoimmunity Test. Keep a graph and chart your score.

_____

_____

_____

_____

_____

_____

_____

_____

_____

_____

_____

_____

_____

_____

_____

_____

_____

_____

    After you have sailed through this joy book, go back and answer the
three pleasure prompters in Chapter Two and retake both of the tests in
this chapter as well. If you regularly take your thirty-minute doses of
delight, take the time to do the SAFE technique and *no'ono'o nui,*
breathe more deeply, chant, and do the *hula,* I promise you that your
scores will go up dramatically. As I suggested earlier, it's very helpful to
ask your family members, co-workers, and friends to take the PQ and
PI tests along with you. You may want to score one another to check for
accuracy. You will find that as your scores rise, the scores of those
around you will rise too.

Chapter Six

Ready, Set … Wait!
Six Welcomes and Six Warnings

E komo mai!
Pronounced "ay ko-mo my"

Welcome!

Like most Hawaiian words, *aloha* has dozens of meanings. Two of them are "hello" and "goodbye." Because Polynesians do not focus on a self always "coming from somewhere" or getting reading to "go somewhere," they require a word that contains the sense of both greeting and departure to signify "just being here." *Aloha* also refers to the sailors' warning "gentle as she goes." Thus *aloha* means to lovingly treasure moments of re-connection, but to not be overly anxious, pushy, or false in our connections. It means to cautiously and judiciously set out and to not be too sad about our goodbyes, because we are heading for new connections and never really disconnecting from our prior ones. And *aloha* refers as well to the fact that every journey of life has its pleasures and perils. We are well advised not to embark too quickly, without attending to both the light and dark side of every life adventure.

Remember that this manual is not intended to be a feel-good book. It is intended to be a "balancing and connecting" book. Healthy pleasure, as we've now learned, is first and foremost daily life balance *(pono)* between loving, working, playing, and healing. In a *pono*-filled life, unhappiness is as natural as happiness, and it helps give happiness meaning and intensity. The word *aloha* captures this balanced idea of living.

One *kahuna* explained this concept to me as follows. "Hello always has some 'hell' in it and every goodbye has some 'good' in it. Slow down and pay attention to your hellos and goodbyes, where you are now, and to whom you are with." In that spirit, here are six welcomes and six warnings for you as you embark upon your life of pleasure.

Six Welcomes and Six Warnings

1. Welcome to the enjoyment of all the health you have!

Despite all the health threats we hear about every day, most people live generally healthy lives. While scientists warn us of dire menaces to our health lurking all around us, the fact is that we now live, on average, thirteen years longer than people did in 1940, and our life expectancy has more than doubled since the start of the twentieth century. Writing pleasure prescriptions for your life is not a matter of trying to avoid getting sick or working hard to comply with every exercise and diet warning. It *is* a matter of living the only life you are likely to have to the fullest, by practicing rational hedonism and reasonable moderation that do not deny you the simple pleasures of life.

I guarantee you that, no matter how long you live, if you follow the pleasure prescriptions offered in this joy book, learn to write your own pleasure prescriptions using these examples, and help others to write their own pleasure prescriptions, you will end up feeling that you have lived long enough and lived exactly the life you wished for. One of my Hawaiian neighbors said, "If you live a *haole* life, you end up with the life you deserve and the hell you were afraid of. If you lead a life of *aloha*, you get the life you dream of and the heaven you hoped for."

Warning! Don't die before you are born!

Everyone dies, but too few of us ever really learn to live. Many of us live our lives fearing death or misfortune. Political scientist Aaron Wildavsky once wrote, "How extraordinary! The richest, longest lived, best protected, most resourceful civilization, with the highest degree of insight into its own technology, is on its way to becoming the most frightened." As you journey into a lifetime of pleasure, you will learn that no one truly lives who does not first accept the fact that he will die. Then you can get busy forgetting that fact, and learn to share a joyful life with others instead of working hard alone to avoid death.

I was surprised and a little embarrassed one day when one of my shyest patients—who has just recovered from three courses of chemotherapy and radiation for "terminal" cancer—told me, "I've learned one thing from all of this. Life is a lot like a penis: how long it is matters a lot less than what you do with it." My warning to you as you begin the journey of joy is this: If all you do is try to live long, your entire life will be spent in endless effort rather than in celebration, and you will never be "born" into a life of true delight.

Of course, just as the Polynesian sailor's journey is dangerous, the joy journey you are about to take won't always be easy. Trying to stop worrying about sickness and early death is challenging. Becoming alert and working hard on healthy ways to live are also challenging tasks. Many in our modern world see pleasure as a mere distraction or temporary reward, so there will be those who question your efforts to find a less hectic, pressured life and even mock you as you take more time to enjoy living. As Shakespeare pointed out, all ships appear calm while in the harbor. But if you are willing to take the risk of setting out to sea and to see, and if you open your heart as well as your mind, you can learn to think, feel, love, work, and play like a Polynesian.

2. Welcome! You are about to have a lot of fun.

The Oceanic Way of cheerful, flowing well-being teaches you a joyous way to love what you have, rather than the Western way of hard work and struggle to get what you want. You know you are not following pleasure prescriptions if you are not having fun putting them into practice and helping others have fun in the process. Pleasure prescriptions always mix silliness, high spirits, cheerfulness, and creativity into their medicine, helping to free your Western brain from its grim and land-locked ways.

Warning! Healthy fun may be dangerous to your illness.

While doctors often talk about risks to our health, pleasure is a risk to any illness. It derives from connection, balance, bliss, good humor, and freedom from time pressure, all of which are very good for your health and very bad for a disease process. Writing pleasure prescriptions requires taking rational behavioral risks, making serious lifestyle changes, balancing work with love and play, sharing reflection and contemplation, drawing, coloring, singing, dancing, listening, praying, and daydreaming. The more childish or even foolish you feel while writing and filling your pleasure prescriptions, the more healthy you and everyone around you will feel and become.

3. Welcome! You are about to learn how to share great pleasure!

One of the most important distinctions between Oceanic and Western thinking is that the Oceanic Way is based on interdependence, not independence. The Western world is a consuming world. It is based on taking the most we can, getting all we can, and "going for it." It stresses standing alone, not standing together. But pleasure prescriptions are written from an Oceanic perspective that says healthy pleasure comes from wanting what we have, having and taking only what we need, helping others have what they need, getting less than we can so others can get more, and being there for others.

Current research clearly shows that those who give the most eventually get the most in terms of better health and more effective healing. The "helper's high" that psychologists write about refers to the neuro-hormonal and immune-system benefits of giving pleasure to others. If you will open your heart to the possibility that the ultimate pleasure comes from giving and sharing pleasure, you will learn to write much more powerful pleasure prescriptions.

Warning! No one can be self-fulfilled!

The Polynesians taught and recent research proves that feelings of disconnection and loneliness are major risks to a healthy and joyful life. Your pleasure prescriptions will become toxic and have negative side effects if they are written only for the self rather than for the world. Remember that the Oceanic Way teaches a kind of pleasure that is quite different from the Western world's concept of pleasure. Polynesian pleasure is a shared and reciprocal experience that brings health and joy to both the pleasurer and those pleasured. If your prescriptions are designed to bring joy and happiness to yourself alone, they will be very weak medicine indeed.

4. Welcome! You are going to learn a simpler way to live!

The more complex our life gets, the less enjoyable it becomes. We may delude ourselves into believing that our cellular phones, beepers, answering machines, fax machines, and other timesaving devices make life more enjoyable, but the fact is that we have less time to enjoy ourselves now than we did before such things were invented.

Our many technical advances allow us more freedom only if we are wise enough to use instead of being used by our technology. Writing pleasure prescriptions requires taking control of the machines that so often seem to control us, by spending more time away from them. A life of pleasure is not a life hemmed in by pager, e-mail, and fax, but a life that includes simple family activities and phone-free strolls through the woods.

A very important step in writing your pleasure prescriptions is to make the time to enjoy life rather than jumping to respond to every beep and ring of the machines that are supposed to work for us.

Warning! There are no gurus!

One of barriers to pleasure in recent times has been the emergence of "how-to-do-it" psycho-gurus who claim to have the latest new program for self achievement. This book, like the Polynesian Way itself, offers no such program, only paths and ways to chart your own course to pleasure, along with the "oldest" new ideas of great minds, from shamans to scientists.

None of the ideas presented here are mine. Just as you do, I struggle daily to make my life, others' lives, and the world a more pleasurable place. The lessons and recommendations in these pages are prescriptions drawn from the hard work, research, and thinking of many scientists, *kahuna*, shamans, and others. I am only a messenger of the ideas that much wiser people have taught me. Any mistakes, exaggerations, and oversimplifications are my responsibility. Any wisdom and creativity are totally the gifts of my teachers.

5. Welcome! You are about to learn how to have less, do less, and say "no."

The way to pleasure is not found by trying to have more, do more, and say "yes" to every opportunity. These are Western paths, not Oceanic routes to healthy joy. As you learn to write and fill pleasure prescriptions, remember that your goal is not to make yourself "better" as an individual, but to "be" completely and fully with everyone and everything, improving life for yourself and those around you.

Warning! You cannot have it all.

Another obstacle to healthy pleasure has been the assumption that we can have it all. The result of this selfish consumerism has been increasing feelings of despair and loss. We miss opportunities to hug a parent, hold a child, or just sit together as a family. We seem willing to spend all of our time for more money, but when we approach our later years, we seem much more willing to give all of our money for more time. If you count your life's worth by personal achievements rather than by shared blissfulness, you will never be like the butterfly who, counting moments instead of months, always has time enough. Pleasure may require some hard choices.

6. Welcome! You are about to learn the joy of being abnormal.

Thomas Moore wrote, "I'd rather be a dysfunctional soul than a well-adjusted robot." What we now consider normal is often really "sick." We are buzzed awake too soon in the morning, bolt down food, rush in near-darkness to and from our jobs, work separated from one another, and return home too tired to love and laugh in leisure with those who matter most. Were we abnormal, we would find the time to spend with our families and make the time for those activities that bring us the most joy.

Warning! Normalcy can be dangerous to your health.

Researchers refer to the Sisyphus Syndrome, named after the mythological king who was condemned, in the afterlife, to forever push an enormous stone up a hill only to watch it fall down again. Too many of us seem to be modern-day Sisyphuses, well-adjusted robots engaging in the "normal" motions of daily living—doing more but enjoying the simple pleasures of life less. The price we pay for normalcy and our Sisyphusian lifestyle is heart disease and cancer. When you write and fill your pleasure prescriptions, you are doing much to reduce your risks for serious illness and maximize your chances for healing when you do become ill.

If you are willing to accept the challenges and warnings presented in this chapter, you will be better able to write your own pleasure prescriptions. If you worry less about early death, focus more on enjoying life now, make your life less of a job and more of a celebration, work to give rather than get pleasure out of life, do without (or at least be much less responsive to) the timesaving devices that take too much of our time, try to have less and say "no" more often, and are willing to be a little "abnormal," you will have opened your mind and heart enough for the Oceanic principles to sink in. You will soon discover that ideas for pleasure prescriptions—creative ideas on how to bring joy into your life and the lives of those around you—begin to pop up more frequently in your surprised, relieved Western mind.

Rested and Ready

In Section One, you have begun to change your mind. You've learned to think like a Polynesian sailor, considered the three pleasure prompters as a starting point for your journey, taken time to catch your breath, done the *hula* for happiness, learned to breathe more deeply, tested your pleasure quotient and your psychoimmunity, stocked up with plenty of the five Cs of *aloha,* and been welcomed and warned about your journey. In Section Two, you'll learn the skills and aptitudes you need to cruise in paradise.

The Three Aptitudes of Healthy Pleasure:

The Joy of Wisdom, Virtue, and Emotional Intelligence

In This Section, You'll Learn

. . . the essential aptitudes and skills of the pleasure navigator, including:

Whether you're wise enough, virtuous enough, and emotionally intelligent enough to live the pleasure-filled life

The connection between wisdom and well-being

The pleasures that a virtuous life brings—and gives to others

Why the successful navigator must know his own emotions, take emotional responsibility, and care for others

Chapter Seven

Are You Shrewd Enough to Celebrate?
Five Ways to Wise Pleasure

Lawe ika maʻalea a kuʻonoʻono
Pronounced "la-vay ee-ka ma ah-lay-ah ah ku oh-no oh-no"

Take wisdom and make it deep

There are three "*aloha* aptitudes" that are essential to writing your plea-sure prescriptions—wisdom, virtue, and emotional intelligence. When the five ingredients of each of these aptitudes, described in the pages that follow, are combined with the five principles of *aloha* (patience, unity, agreeableness, humbleness, and kindness), the result is fifteen ways in which the *mana* necessary for writing your pleasure prescrip-tions can be summoned.

This chapter helps you understand the wisdom necessary for a pleasurable life, and Chapters Eight and Nine discuss virtue and emo-tional intelligence respectively. Each chapter presents a test that will help you assess your current levels of each of these aptitudes. The last chapter of this section, Chapter Ten, summarizes and integrates *aloha*, wisdom, virtue, and emotional intelligence into a fifteen-item menu for writing *mana*-filled pleasure prescriptions. You may wish to take the tests in these chapters now and return to them once more after completing the book in order to assess your progress. Writing space can be found at the end of each of these chapters, and you can record your progress there.

Wisdom and Well-Being

The word *wisdom* is defined in *Webster's Third New International Dictionary* as the personification of God's will in the creation of the world. It is the accumulated lore of a culture and grows out of the instinctive adaptations of those who create that culture. Wisdom is distinct from smartness and intelligence. Human beings—the earth's smartest species—are getting smarter and smarter but not wiser and wiser, and as a result, we seem to have more but are able to enjoy life less.

It is wisdom, not intelligence, that helps us find meaning and pleasure in life. Harvard psychologist Jerome Kagan notes that intelligence helped us make an atomic bomb, but wisdom helps us know not to use it and to wonder why we made it in the first place. Author and editor Bennett Cerf wrote that wisdom is available at negligible cost to all of us within the covers of books, but wisdom is much more than what we can learn by reading. It is a way of thinking and being based on much the same concepts that make up *aloha*, and a major reason for our delight deficiency is the fact that most of us don't have enough wisdom to lead sensible and sensitive lives. As one *kupuna* (pronounced "ku-pu-nah" and meaning "Hawaiian elder") told me, "There seem to be an awful lot of very unhappy smart people, but I seldom see a very unhappy wise person."

The Polynesian concept of wisdom is based on the lessons of the ancestors. Unlike the Western view of intelligence, which places emphasis on written symbols, words, numbers, and logic, Hawaiians approach problems first from the perspective of ancient lessons and stories that illustrate the best way to maintain connection with the land, God, and the family system. To be smart in the West is to be up-to-date and to know the latest and newest ideas. To be wise in Polynesia is to remember the oldest and most tested ways of living in deep respect for others and for the earth.

The concept of wisdom has been studied by Dr. Paul Baltes and his associates at the Max Planck Institute for Human Development and Education. By presenting moral dilemmas and assessing the ways in which people deal with these problems, Baltes has identified five basic characteristics of wisdom, which are incorporated into the test given in this chapter.

Baltes' work indicates that wisdom requires a fivefold orientation to life. First, we must be composed enough to realize that overreaction to life's stressful situations is destructive. Secondly, we must be able to view events in a realistic framework, one that acknowledges the natural and necessary chaos of life. Third, we must avoid our natural tendency to be suspicious of or defensive toward others—a destructive gift of our evolution. Fourth, we must not expect things always to turn out the way we want them to; we must be willing to adjust to the way things actually are. Finally, we must remember that, despite our human-centered assumption that people are in charge of the world, we're not: everyone's life falls victim to the random jokes, little hassles, and big accidents of the universe.

One of my Hawaiian *kumu* (teacher) friends from the Big Island of Hawai'i summed up Baltes' research for me, combining it with her Oceanic knowledge of *aloha* pleasure. She said, "If you're going to be telling Westerners about wise pleasure, be sure to tell them that they are often too stressed, too narrow in their views of life, too hot-headed and overreactive, too controlling, and expect too much out of life. They seem to feel entitled to have pleasure rather than working to deserve and earn it through a gentle life of profound respect for the *'aina*, *'ohana* [family], and *na kupuna*. They live too much for immediate pleasure and don't realize that pleasure is like the ocean. We all enjoy swimming in it and surfing on the waves, but its pleasure is not ours alone, and we cannot control it. Good surfers help the other surfers and wait for a wave to come along to share."

To help you learn the way of wise pleasure, take the Wisdom for Pleasure Test offered below. The five ways of wisdom that this test focuses on are much like those that Baltes isolated in his research. Your score will help you understand how well you are practicing the characteristics of balanced wisdom in your own life as you face the daily dilemmas of the modern world.

First, a note on the test itself: Ho'ala Hou has collected more than 1,000 scores on the tests in Chapters Seven, Eight, and Nine, including scores from both Western and Polynesian people. Wherever I have traveled in Polynesia, or whenever I have met Polynesians in my travels, their natural generosity has permitted me to collect their scores on these tests ("Western"-ized though the tests may be), and to gain their insight into the sacred and ancient beliefs of Polynesia. In my testing, I of course make no claim that these very simple inventories can come close to capturing the profound nature of the Polynesian peoples and the Oceanic Way.

The average scores from Polynesians that I have included in these chapters are drawn from a group of 100 *kupuna*. I have attended seminars with and learned much from these elders. Together, we've made floral *lei,* smoothed *ipu,* carved fish hooks, and "talked story" together about the question of healthy pleasure, Polynesian-style. These *kupuna* volunteered to take the tests in these chapters in order to help share their wisdom about Oceanic well-being with the world. For comparative purposes, their test scores are given along with each test in these chapters.

THE WISDOM FOR PLEASURE TEST

SCORING

0 = Never

1 = Almost Never

2 = Sometimes

3 = Often

4 = Very Often

5 = Always

Do You Reflect Calmly?

_____ Are you patient *(ahonui)* enough to wait for an entire problem to be exposed before you try to deal with it?

_____ Do you think that you have a basic factual knowledge about life and the fundamentals of healthy daily living?

_____ Are you willing to look at the full scope, range, and depth of issues before you begin to solve or deal with them?

_____ Do you avoid "prolepsis," addressing problems or confronting arguments before they are entirely presented?

Are You Alert to Context?

_____ Are you in sufficient harmony *(lokahi)* with your world to see all sides to an issue?

_____ Are you free of "presentism" and able to look at problems from a far-ranging perspective, rather than just considering them in the here and now?

_____ Are you alert to your surroundings, clearly observing what is going on around you?

_____ Are you a synthesizer, trying to put things together rather than categorizing, separating, and stratifying people and reality?

Do You Consider Rather than React?

_____ Are you agreeable *('olu'olu)* enough to slow down and think things out before responding?

_____ Do you avoid responding in a defensive or overly assertive manner?

_____ Do you try your best to apply a studied, considered, kind, tolerant viewpoint to problems?

_____ Do you assess the costs and benefits to yourself and others when you come up with solutions to problems?

Do You Respect Uncertainty?

_____ Would other people say that you are humble and modest *(ha'aha'a)*, rather than a know-it-all?

_____ Are you secure enough to acknowledge your uncertainties and the fact that nothing in life is "for sure"?

_____ Do you easily and freely accept criticism without getting defensive?

_____ Do you accept that there is no perfect solution to any problem and that there are numerous ways to approach any problem?

Do You Value Relativism?

_____ Would others who know you well say that you are kind and tender *(akahai)* enough to easily accept values that are far from your own?

_____ Do you work hard to understand others' ways of thinking and conclusions?

_____ Do you avoid judging others' ideas as less valuable than your own?

_____ Do you try to learn from others, no matter how far out their thinking, values, and life priorities seem to you?

TOTAL WISDOM FOR PLEASURE SCORE _____

Interpreting Your Wisdom for Pleasure Score

Based on the research of Ho'ala Hou and our testing and interviews with Hawaiians and hundreds of other persons around the world, consider your score in terms of the following scale.

90–100: A Western *kupuna*
You're wise enough to share and enjoy life with others.
(The average *kupuna* scored 91 on this test.)

80–89: A *kupuna* in the making
You're shrewd, but you need to be wiser in order to experience more shared joy.

70–79: Western *kupuna* potential, but a lot of change needed
You're smart, but not wise enough to get full pleasure out of living.

69 or below: A *keiki* (child) in need of learning
You're too mentally rushed and rash to fully enjoy life.

Intelligence is knowing what to look out for, but wisdom is knowing what to overlook. Where intelligence is fast, wisdom is reflective. Where intelligence focuses, wisdom seeks context. Where intelligence requires rapid reaction and quick thinking, wisdom requires measured consideration and delayed responses. Where intelligence seeks certainty, wisdom teaches that nothing is certain. Intelligence strives for confidence and clarity, but wisdom is based on the recognition that the world is naturally chaotic and everything is relative. Intelligence helps us cope with the modern world, but wisdom helps us *make* a better world. Intelligence helps us achieve, but wisdom helps us learn how to joyfully use our achievements together, and in the process make life a pleasure.

If you want to work toward becoming a Western *kupuna*—a wiser person searching for balanced pleasure—use the space below to write down some answers to the following questions. As you write, ask yourself whether you've really taken the time to calmly reflect upon situations and problems before dealing with them, and whether you've worked for wisdom and calm.

1. A recent, major problem that upset me was:

2. In dealing with this problem, I think I acted:

3. My family thought that I acted:

4. Based on what I've read so far, I know that there are different ways to deal with my problem. If I were a *kupuna,* here's how I might have handled this problem:

_____

_____

_____

_____

5. (To be done after you're answered the above questions): Hawaiians look less to the head than to the heart (*pu'uwai,* pronounced "poo oo-vi") in the quest for balanced problem-solving. My next book, titled *The Heart's Code: New Findings About Cellular Memories and their Role in the Mind, Body, Spirit Connection* (New York: Broadway Books, to be published in April 1998), presents ways to use the wisdom of the loving heart, rather than the cleverness of the selfish brain, to deal with the pressures of modern life.

Chapter Eight

Do You Deserve a Pleasurable Life?
Five Ways to Virtuous Pleasure

Ua kuluma ke kanaka i ke aloha
Pronounced "oo-ah ku-lew-ma kay ka-nah-ka ee kay ah-lo-ha"

"Love is a customary virtue with man," meaning that any woman or man, if wise enough, can find love in anyone, anywhere, at any time

The word *virtue* is defined in *Webster's Third New International Dictionary* as moral practice or action and conformity to a standard of rightness. Virtue means seeking to lead a life for and in compliance with the highest good. Tutu Mama, the highly respected Hawaiian *kupuna* and dear friend who gave me my Hawaiian name, told me, "Ka'ikena, always teach your own students to be nice. Teach them about virtue. Even if they are very smart or even very wise, their lives will not bring pleasure to others if they do not have virtue to bring their wisdom alive. If they do not bring pleasure to others, they will never find joy in their own lives."

A key component of *aloha* is *akahai*, kindness practiced with tenderness. In the simplest terms, persons showing *akahai* are nice people who make life a pleasure for everyone around them. For Hawaiians, doing the right thing and doing nice things for people and the world is not just the right thing to do, but the healthy way to live. Another meaning of *pono* is "righteousness," and for Hawaiians, virtue means living every day to help bring the world and the *'aina* into balance in accordance with the ancient virtues and principles of their culture.

Virtuous pleasure requires a steady heart, meaning that one does not avoid doing the right thing, even when doing it is very difficult. It requires treating everyone as family, not just those who live in our house, but those who live with us in this world. It requires being the sort of person whose *mana* seems to attract others and to whom others easily turn for help, comfort, or direction. It requires being alert to one's affect on others and always being aware that words have immense spiritual power.

When I tried to measure the sacred and complex aspects of Polynesian virtue in a Westernized test, I asked the *kupuna* of Hawai'i to help me. They warned me, first of all, that real pleasure takes into account the pleasure of others. To pursue selfish pleasure is seen in Polynesia as a show of disrespect not only for the people now alive in the world, but for the ancestors by whose grace and love one is allowed the joy of living.

One 92-year-old *kupuna* told me: "If you have pleasure in your life, you must be like the fisherman who shares his fortune and respects its source and its limits. You have to be strong enough to always be ready to help others have pleasure. You must think first if your pleasure in any way prevents another person from having pleasure now or later, and then remember not to be too loud or obvious about your own joy, just in case someone else is not feeling as joyful as you at that moment. When people are sad, they are expressing your sad side for you at that moment, just as you are expressing their happy side for them at that moment. You must remember not to get carried away with your pleasure and to only sample a little of it, just like a fisherman takes only the fish he needs, shares his fish with others first, and does not tell everyone how good a fisherman he is. You must remember to be fair in your pleasure and to show your appreciation to your ancestors by *pule* [prayer], thanking them, and being very sure to give back to the *'aina* whenever you have taken from it." (This *kupuna*, like the others who talked with me, spoke in Hawaiian, so my translation here must be seen as only an approximation of the wisdom of his words.)

Based on the teachings of both modern psychology and ancient Polynesia, virtuous pleasure may be seen as containing five elements. First, it means sticking patiently with a problem, even when giving up would be easier. Secondly, it means being vigilant to the pleasure of others. Third, it means overcoming the Western myth that one must love oneself before loving others. Fourth, it means refraining from displays of one's pleasure through brashness and showing off, and instead modeling graceful, humble appreciation of those times when good fortune visits and remembering that nothing very good (or very bad) ever lasts. And it means, finally, being sure that one's pleasure never deprives another person of pleasure.

The following Virtuous Pleasure Test helps you assess the degree to which you are basically a nice person, one who is virtuous in all areas of life. As with all of the tests in this book, I've designed its items based on the latest research and writings about healthy pleasure by Western psychologists and scientists, along with the basic *aloha* principles of Polynesia.

THE VIRTUOUS PLEASURE TEST

SCORING

0 = Never

1 = Almost Never

2 = Sometimes

3 = Often

4 = Very Often

5 = Always

Do You Model Fortitude?

_____ Are you patient *(ahonui)* enough to stand by your friends even when their problems make you feel uncomfortable or you feel they have brought their problems on themselves?

_____ Do you try to do the right thing even when doing it is very difficult for you?

_____ Do you avoid making threats to quit, give up, or leave in the face of problems?

_____ Would others say that you can be counted on even in the toughest of times?

Do You Express Compassion?

_____ Are you connected *(lokahi)* enough with others to always get along, no matter how difficult people may be?

_____ Do you extend to strangers the same courtesy and civility that you show to your family?

_____ Do you easily cry when you see or hear about a stranger's loss?

_____ Do you consider the world's problems your problems and responsibilities?

Are You Temperate?

_____ How often do other people say that you are a very pleasant *('olu'olu)* person?

_____ Do you show good self-discipline, expressed by eating right, exercising as you feel you should, and avoiding unhealthy behaviors?

_____ Do you avoid having "life secrets"—secrets about your most private personal behavior in work, play, or love that, if made public, would embarrass you or your family?

_____ Do you easily say "no" to opportunities even when you feel very lucky, honored, or tempted by the challenge and chance?

Are You Prudent?

_____ Would others say that you are a very humble, modest *(ha'aha'a)* person?

_____ Would others say that you are a cautious, careful person?

_____ Do you obey all traffic laws and comply with the rules of society even if you do not agree with them?

_____ Would others say that you are a discreet person who can keep a secret and does not gossip about other people?

Are You a Just Person?

_____ Would others say that you are a very kind and gentle *(akahai)* person?

_____ Would others say that you are a very fair person?

_____ Would others say that you never lie and can be completely trusted?

_____ Do you enjoy serving others—giving help and assistance without expecting rewards, acknowledgment, or reciprocation from the people whom you've served?

TOTAL VIRTUOUS PLEASURE SCORE _____

Interpreting Your Virtuous Pleasure Score

Based on Ho'ala Hou research and testing, here is a scale to help you put your virtue score in perspective.

90–100: Highly virtuous
You make others' lives very happy and therefore can expect a great deal of pleasure in return. (The average *kupuna* scored 93 on this test.)

80–89: A little less than virtuous
You are less than reliable when it comes to creating a joyful life for others.

79–80: Virtues slipping
Others cannot rely on you as a consistent source of healthy pleasure in their lives, and your own pleasure is also diminished.

78 or below: Virtues slipping badly
The misery you sometimes bring to others blocks not only their joy but your own healthy pleasure.

Every child has heard the words "be nice." It does little good to be a very wise person if you do not extend the value of that wisdom by behaving in a caring, gentle, helpful, forgiving, moral way. Furthermore, being nice can actually improve your health. Research in psychoneuroimmunology (PNI), as I've said earlier in this book, clearly indicates that giving, caring, connecting people tend to get sick less and to heal faster when they do get sick. The body and brain seem to sense the value of virtuous treatment of others and show their appreciation through the good physical feelings we enjoy when we behave nicely. PNI research shows that the basic qualities of virtuous pleasure, when cultivated and developed, enhance your immune power. The cells in your body that identify substances that threaten your health actually begin to behave in a more virtuous way when you think and act virtuously.

When my own patients suffer, I help them learn some of the Polynesian virtuous-pleasure paths to healing—namely fortitude, compassion, temperance, prudence, and justness. I remind them not to be just receivers of healing, but senders of healing (and thus practice fortitude). I tell them to call sick friends and to visit other patients in the hospital even when they themselves are feeling weak. When my patients do so, they almost always report a boost in energy. I ask them to practice compassion by avoiding getting angry with hospital staff, even when the routines of the hospital are infuriating. I warn them not to overdo their symptoms or play the martyr, even when they have every reason to do so. I also warn them not to always try for a positive attitude—and somewhere in between these two poles of martyrdom and false cheerfulness, they discover temperance. I remind them that I too suffered through cancer, chemotherapy, and a bone-marrow transplant, and that everyone suffers eventually: sometimes it is just "our turn." I invite my patients to be fair and understanding of those who seem to take health and good fortune for granted, for they too will have their opportunities to suffer, heal, and become whole again—and thus my patients practice prudence and learn about justness.

Finally, I give them the very good news that each of these behaviors has been proven by PNI research to enhance the immune system, and thus that they've embarked on a particularly powerful path to healing. When it comes to the value of virtue, I remind them, PNI shows that "Do unto others as you would have your immune system do unto you" is the golden rule of a healthy and pleasurable life.

If your virtuous pleasure score is less than you'd hoped, however, remember to deal with that news in a virtuously pleasurable way. That means you need to keep trying to change those items that lowered your score, trying to bring pleasure to others, cultivating the self-discipline necessary to not give up, and trying to be modest enough to remember that you should not expect too much of yourself. Remember that your virtuous pleasure potential is as limitless as any other person's, and remember to be fair with yourself and recognize that each time you take this test (or the other tests in this book), you're only sampling your mind at one point in time. There's plenty of opportunity for change.

Remember as well that just a small improvement in any of the items on this test will pay big dividends in terms of your mental and physical health. As one of the *kupuna,* who felt she'd scored too low on this test, told me: "It's like making a *lei.* Just because you mess up doesn't mean that you throw the *lei* away. You stop, take a breath, say a *pule,* and promise yourself and your ancestors that you will try just a little harder, but not a lot harder. If you don't do that, you only get less pleasure from life, because you did not stay patient with yourself."

Below, you'll find some space that you can use to do your own writing about virtuous pleasure. Here are some questions that will help you focus your mind and generate ideas about what you can do to bring true virtue into your life.

1. Describe the time in your life when you were most ill. Describe the place, the time, and how you felt—not only physically, but mentally and spiritually.

---

2. Next, describe how you think you made others feel during this time.

_____

_____

_____

3. What lessons did you learn about yourself while you were sick?

_____

_____

_____

_____

_____

4. Now that you're feeling better, and now that you've learned more about virtuous pleasure, what do you think you could have done differently in order to enhance your healing potential?

_____

_____

_____

_____

5. Based on what you've learned about virtuous pleasure, what would you do to help a friend or family member who became ill?

_____

_____

_____

_____

Chapter Nine

Do You Have Sensible Sentiments?
Five Ways to Emotionally
Intelligent Pleasure

E wehe i ka umauma i akea
Pronounced "ee vay-hay ee ka oo-mah-oo-ma ee ah-key-ah"

"Open the chest that it may be spacious," meaning be
generous and kind to all

Author Daniel Goleman, in his book *Emotional Intelligence,* distinguishes between intellectual competence and the ability to be sensitive to, moderate, and match one's emotional state with one's environment. He says that bringing thoughtfulness to our emotions and not allowing ourselves to succumb to the territoriality, defensiveness, and hyperreactivity of the lower levels of our brains is essential to the survival of our world. If we are captive to our fight-or-flight lower instincts, life becomes a constant war of survival and self-protection rather than a shared pleasure.

According to Goleman, a person who is emotionally intelligent is someone alert to her emotional impact on others. She's someone who can calm herself down and realize that a person or event has not "made her angry," that she has a choice as to how she will make herself feel. Emotional intelligence means being emotionally "with it" rather than reactively "out of it."

Being able to read, acknowledge, understand, and deal with one's own and others' emotions is crucial to a life of affective (emotional) and mental balance—the *pono* that is essential to healthy pleasure. When we are affectively reactive instead of emotionally literate, we become disconnected from others, and that always leads to displeasure. Being emotionally literate means that we can read and react appropriately to others' feelings, allowing us to share with them the joys of living rather than spending our time defending ourselves. It's no fun being angry and it's not fun when someone is angry with us, so a pleasurable life is one based on being able to calm down, recognize how we and others are feeling, and remain patient *(ahonui)* and agreeable *('olu'olu)* enough to stay connected with others.

In Hawaii, as we've discovered, the word *pono* means more than just balance. It also refers to living in a less reactive, calmer, less impulsive way, and thus *pono* relates directly to Goleman's concept of emotional intelligence. *Pono* means trying to live in terms of the way things are supposed to be, the way that *Akua* (God) intends them to be. Someone living in *pono* not only lives a balanced life with her *'ohana,* the *'aina,* and her *na kupuna,* but also works every day to help her community and the world live in *pono.* In the Oceanic model, psychological, spiritual, and physical health is not an individual accomplishment—it is a result of the lifelong process of helping the world into balance and "rightness." Real health means emotionally intelligent living, blended with spiritual integrity and respect for the world.

On the next page you'll find the Emotional Literacy Test used by Ho'ala Hou in its research into this key aspect of healthy joy. It tests for the five components of emotional intelligence, drawing both upon Goleman's work and the concepts of *aloha* pleasure. Emotional intelligence means being less emotionally reactive and less emotionally dependent on others' emotional states. It also means being alert to and understanding of how other people, animals, and (at least in Polynesia) objects feel. It means taking emotional responsibility, saying "I've gotten myself upset" rather than "You made me angry." It means knowing how you feel before your feelings boil over and burn other people. Finally, it means abandoning the current Western way of "doing unto others because they have done unto you" and practicing the real golden rule at work, home, and play.

THE EMOTIONAL LITERACY TEST

SCORING

0 = Never

1 = Almost Never

2 = Sometimes

3 = Often

4 = Very Often

5 = Always

Do You Manage Your Emotions?

_____ Are you patient*(ahonui)* enough to avoid quickly getting angry?

_____ Do you easily and quickly calm yourself down after conflicts rather than ruminating over and reliving angry events?

_____ Do you realize that no matter how bad things get, they will get better, and that no matter how good things are, they can easily get worse?

_____ Would others say that you have a very cool head in working, loving, and playing?

Do You Empathize Freely?

_____ Are you connected *(lokahi)* enough with life to be aware that everything you do or say has an emotional impact?

_____ Would others say that you are able to feel exactly what they are feeling?

_____ Would others say that you are a very sensitive person who does not want to hurt anyone's feelings, even when you think someone may deserve it?

_____ Are children, animals, and complete strangers easily and quickly drawn to you?

Do You Take Emotional Responsibility?

_____ Are you agreeable *('olu'olu)* enough to avoid conflicts whenever possible, rather than defending your turf?

_____ Would others say that you are very difficult to anger and very easygoing?

_____ In disagreements, do you avoid saying things like "She made me angry" and "Look what you made me do?"

_____ Would others say that you are not someone who "gets his anger out"—via yelling, rages, or tantrums—and that you wait and let your anger dissipate? (See the table on the next page for more information on anger.)

Do You Know Your Own Emotions?

_____ Would others say that you are modest and humble *(ha'aha'a)* enough to be clearly aware of your own emotions and their impact on others?

_____ Would others say that you're well in control of your emotions?

_____ Would the person closest to you in your life say that you are tuned in to your feelings and easily express and share them?

_____ Do others easily approach you and tell you their feelings without fear of upsetting or angering you?

Do You Sympathize Openly?

_____ Would others say that you are kind*(akahai)* enough to not only empathize (acknowledge others' feelings) but to accept their feelings without judgment?

_____ Would others say that you refrain from making value judgments about people's feelings?

_____ Would the person closest to you in your life say that you are more than willing to talk at length about feelings without rushing to "do something about them" or "solve the problem"?

_____ Consider your own emotional nature. Would you feel very comfortable, free, and safe living with you every day?

TOTAL EMOTIONAL LITERACY SCORE _____

A Profile of Anger

Humans are the angriest of animals and anger is probably one of our oldest emotions. Anger is one reason human beings and not some gentler animal dominates the planet. The great danger in anger is the seductive effectiveness in delivering a sense of short-term victory and protection of one's perceived territory. Unfortunately, to the victor also goes the heart bypass. . . .

There are three components of hostility that put us at risk for illness and loss of pleasure. The word hostility refers to malevolence, unfriendliness, antagonism, and feeling that other people are the enemy. Polynesians call hostility *paio*, which means a way of thinking, feeling, and behaving that does not bring joy to anyone and is composed of mental, emotional, and physical experiences of anger.

Hostility is a dangerous combination of cynicism, anger, and aggression. It includes a distrusting attitude, an agitated and defensive emotional state, and the aggressive expression of these thoughts and feelings through internal and external language and behaviors. In short, hostility can be seen as revenge against yourself the mistakes of others.

—from *The Pleasure Prescription*

Interpreting Your Emotional Literacy Score

From Ho'ala Hou research data, here is a scale to help you put your own emotional literacy score in perspective.

90–100: Excellent emotion reader
(The average *kupuna*'s score on the Emotional Literacy Test was 92.)

80–89: Slight emotion-reading disability
Others may find you a little difficult.

70–79: Severe emotion-reading disability
Others may not tell you so, but you make sharing a joyful life very difficult.

69 or below: Emotional dyslexia
You're making life pretty unpleasant for a lot of people.

Perhaps the greatest danger to the survival of our world is our lack of emotional intelligence. The Western world believes emotions are reflexive and involuntary. The Oceanic Way argues that all emotions are choices. Polynesians rarely say, "I just couldn't help myself" or "Now look what you've done to me." Instead they say, "I've made myself feel badly" or "Now look how upset I've gotten myself." Polynesians know that when we feel angry, we must have planted the seed of that anger. We are not the hapless victims of our emotions, but the harvesters of the sentiment-seeds we sow. As simple as it sounds, Polynesians find more pleasure in life because they strongly believe in the concept of reciprocal rebound—what goes around, comes around.

You can use the space below to record your progress in and thoughts about emotional intelligence.

Chapter Ten

A Menu for Fun-Based Fitness:
The Fifteen "Fun-damentals"
of Healthy Pleasure

When you combine wisdom, virtue, and emotional intelligence with the five elements of *aloha*, the result is fifteen ingredients that, in varying combinations, make up the "fun-damentals" of pleasure prescriptions. You can apply these fun-damentals to your loving, working, playing, and healing.

Here is the list. Keep it handy and use it as a checklist for keeping your pleasure prescriptions in a wise, virtuous, emotionally intelligent balance.

THE FUN-DAMENTALS OF PLEASURE CHECKLIST

Ahonui: Patience, Expressed with Perseverance

1. _____ Wisdom: Am I calmly reflecting and taking the time to listen to messages from my soul, rather than yielding to my brain's striving for personal success?

2. _____ Virtue: Am I modeling fortitude, avoiding cynical surrender, and remembering that adversity can be the catalyst for growth?

3. _____ Emotional Intelligence: Am I remaining composed and not letting my emotions manage me?

Lokahi: Unity, Expressed Harmoniously

4. _____ Wisdom: Am I staying alert to context and remembering that the present is only one-third of the moment—recognizing that every moment also contains the past and the future?

5. _____ Virtue: Am I regularly showing compassion at home, at work, and at play, and trying to extend that caring to everyone regardless of their status?

6. _____ Emotional Intelligence: Am I staying tuned in to the emotions involved in all of my interactions and remembering that all relationships—at work, at home, and at play—are first and foremost emotional connections?

'Olu'olu: Agreeableness, Expressed with Pleasantness

7. _____ Wisdom: Am I avoiding "just reacting" and saying things like "they make me angry" or "he or she made me upset"?

8. _____ Virtue: Am I remembering to be temperate and realizing that I always have a choice and don't have to yield to my passions and appetites?

9. _____ Emotional Intelligence: Am I staying emotionally responsible, apologizing when I should, and realizing how I make others feel?

Ha'aha'a: Humbleness, Expressed with Modesty

10. _____ Wisdom: Am I realizing and respecting life's uncertainty rather than complaining, grumbling, griping, whining, and grousing?

11. _____ Virtue: Am I trying to be prudent by saying less, listening more, and saying "no" when I know that saying "yes" would deprive me of my family time?

12. _____ Emotional Intelligence: Am I avoiding taking things personally, seeing negative events as symbolic of my life, and viewing bad things that happen to me as permanent?

Akahai: Kindness, Expressed with Tenderness

13. _____ Wisdom: Am I acting as if everything is relative and considering and accepting others' unique values and beliefs?

14. _____ Virtue: Am I staying free of secrets that do not make me proud, and am I behaving honorably, fairly, honestly, and in a way that would make my ancestors and descendants very, very proud?

15. _____ Emotional Intelligence: Am I a very nice person, keeping most of my emotional expressions toward others cordial, kind, tactful, considerate, and polite?

Add any fun-damentals you think belong to this list in the space below. Then keep checking back on your fun-damentals of pleasure list as you take the sixty pleasure prescriptions that follow in the next section of this book.

_____

_____

_____

_____

_____

_____

_____

_____

_____

The Pleasure Prescriptions:

Sixty Ways to Create Joyous Loving, Gratifying Working, Hearty Playing, and Jubilant Healing

In This Section, You'll

. . . embark on the journey into pleasure, using and writing pleasure prescriptions for:

Joyous loving, including healthy voyeurism, soothing sensuality, loving from the outside in, and learning the art of wish-craft

Gratifying working, including knowing when to give up, valuing your values, pleasurable pacing, and just saying "maybe"

Hearty playing, including messing around, playing without scores, and treating your hardening of the attitudes

Jubilant healing, including restorative grace, re-energizing grit, doing "denial distractions," looking on the dark side, throwing "pity parties," and praying

And you'll learn to write your own prescriptions, creating wise medicine for a lifetime of pleasure.

Chapter Eleven

Aloha Pumehana (Warm Loving): Fifteen Prescriptions for Joyous Loving

Aloha mai no, aloha aku
Pronounced slowly as "ah-lo-ha ma-ee no, ah-lo-ha ah-koo"

When love is given, love should be returned

The pleasure prescriptions that follow are organized around the five basic components of *aloha*. Following a description of each *aloha* principle, I'll present several "fun-damentals," brief statements that combine the *aloha* principle with related concepts of wisdom, virtue, and emotional intelligence. A pleasure prescription that puts the *aloha* principle and fun-damental together in a plan of action is then presented.

At the end of this book, there is a chapter that shows you, using the prescriptions you will read, how to write your own pleasure prescriptions. The "template" for your prescriptions should follow the format of the sixty prescriptions presented earlier. Based perhaps on some of the tests you have taken so far, you'll identify an *aloha* principle you would like to practice in your own life, state it as a simple fun-damental, and then design your own behavioral plan for putting that *aloha* pleasure principle into practice.

Here are fifteen pretested prescriptions for more pleasurable loving. Each has been used for years by my patients, students, and people in organizations for which I have consulted, bringing greater, warmer loving into their lives.

Ahonui Aloha (Loving Patience)

Pleasurable loving ultimately depends on what I call a "forbearance of fondness," in which we patiently tolerate the flaws each of us brings to an intimate relationship and allow plenty of time for love to grow, mature, and struggle through the essential ups and downs of the process of making a life bond. One *kahuna* said, "You would not plant taro and then yell at it to grow faster. If you are patient, you can enjoy watching it grow, and then you can grow with it. You learn that it grows as fast as it has to and as slow as it must to become full of that which gives it its strength and allows it to share its strength with you." And so it is with love.

Wise Loving: Learn the value of "overlooking" flaws and looking for loving potential

PLEASURE PRESCRIPTION 1.

Try a little healthy voyeurism

Set aside some time each month to "look with love." When someone you care deeply about is distracted by a book or television, study that person. Look carefully at that person's eyes, mouth, hair, posture, and mannerisms.

When we lose someone close to us, one of our deepest regrets is often that we have not taken enough time to fix that person's image in our mind and heart. One of my patients who lost her husband said, "I just wish I could look at him alive one more time, and this time really drink him in." A mother told me, "My children grew so quickly and we were always so busy. I just wish I would have taken more time to really see them as children instead of always being so busy doing things for and with them." The "look with love" pleasure prescription is one way to get a fix on those persons whom you want to imprint on your soul. Don't miss your chance.

You can use the space provided below to record your "look with love" impressions.

_____

_____

Virtuous Loving: Lasting loving is as much grit as grace

PLEASURE PRESCRIPTION 2.

Keep a Saturday list

In many ways, all families are dysfunctional and codependent. All intimate relationships go through periods of crisis and conflict. During heated moments of dissension, it can seem that your entire relationship is negative. The very good times can be forgotten or clouded when the very closeness of a relationship causes friction that heats up interactions. Pleasure Prescription 2 is designed to add a little grit to the grace of loving.

Whenever a problem occurs, write the problem on a Saturday list. Everyone involved should write his or her description of the problem on a single piece of paper. Keep the list in a very noticeable place—such as on the refrigerator or on a family bulletin board. Some of my patients tape-record the list for playing back on Saturday, and others store their list on the family computer or voice mail. Set aside one time every Saturday to take up the problems on the list. You will most likely find that many of the problems have solved themselves, are no longer important, or even seem not to have been problems at all, after time for calm reflection has toned them down.

As you go over your Saturday list, reflect on the fact that the strength of your loving often soothes and anesthetizes the pain of conflicts. Each time new problems occur, remember that loving has fortitude and an endurance all its own and can heal by itself if we don't let our selfish brains get involved in fighting for territory or casting blame. The Saturday list can teach your relationship grit, reminding you that most problems are nowhere near as important as they seemed in the heat of the moment, and that a relationship usually has much more strength and adaptability than we think. We need only give it the gift of time.

Emotionally Intelligent Loving: "Hot" love burns out, but warm loving nurtures

PLEASURE PRESCRIPTION 3.

Try a little soothing sensuality

Western culture is a "hot" culture. We seem to prefer the new, intense, different, fast, and extreme over the old, gentle, same, slow, and predictable. Pleasure Prescription 3 is designed to help you "cool down your loving" so that you and your lover can warm up one another's hearts.

Set aside one "passion pause" time per month. Spend that time holding, touching, feeling, and listening to music together. Don't talk, don't have sex, just connect in a soothing, gentle way.

Record your thoughts about your passion pauses here.

_____

_____

_____

_____

_____

_____

_____

_____

_____

_____

_____

Lokahi Aloha (Harmonious Loving)

A relationship that brings pleasure to its participants is one that is designed to make the world a happier place, not just to make those in the relationship happier.

Wise Loving: Know the person you are most intimately connected with, so that she or he is a more central part of your daily thoughts and feelings

PLEASURE PRESCRIPTION 4.

See your whole lover

Draw a "lover's portrait" that fully describes the person you are closest to. This description should answer six questions, and each should be fully completed. Record your answers in the spaces provided.

1. What does this person think about a lot in his or her life?

2. How does this person usually feel on a day-to-day basis?

3. How does this person spend his or her time when no one else is around?

4. What is this person's greatest hope?

5. What is this person's greatest fear?

6. How have you contributed to who and how this person is?

Put this lover's portrait in the form of a letter, send it to the person you care about, and ask him or her whether you were correct in your answers. Doing so helps you put your lover in his or her full context. It also helps the person you love consider how you view him or her and allows for corrections and clarifications.

Virtuous Loving: Showing loving care to complete strangers strengthens your "love-ability"

PLEASURE PRESCRIPTION 5.

Try some stranger love

Our culture so romanticizes love that we embrace the ideals of a "one and only" and "family first." But healthy pleasure requires a deep sense of connection with everyone and everything. This fifth pleasure prescription helps you broaden and strengthen your compassion, and the result is not only a better world, but loving benefits to yourself and your family from your growing and expanding compassion.

Set aside about half as much time per week as you spend in working out or exercising. Spend that time volunteering. Work in a soup kitchen or help out at school or at the hospital. Be sure you actually do something to help a stranger, don't just send a check. Showing your compassion for strangers is not only a virtue; it strengthens your loving skills, makes you more lovable, and has been shown to strengthen your immunity. You can record your experiences—or write down more ideas for your stranger love—below.

Emotionally Intelligent Loving: Empathy inspires love and lovers

PLEASURE PRESCRIPTION 6.

Keep a feelings file

One of the most joyful experiences of being alive is not only feeling a range of emotions but feeling the emotions of others. The following prescription is designed to help increase your loving empathy.

Keep a diary of the feelings of the person closest to you emotionally. Instead of writing about your own feelings in your own diary, make brief daily entries about how you sense that a person who matters a lot to you feels. Try to be at least as clear about the feelings of your loved one as you are about your own feelings. You can begin your diary here—but eventually you'll want to acquire a special notebook or journal for your feelings file.

_____

_____

_____

_____

_____

'Olu'olu Aloha (Agreeable Loving)

One of the most neglected aspects of joyful loving is politeness to those who matter most. When we behave and speak politely and lovingly, we begin to feel more love. Love is not just emotional; it is volitional. While psychology has taught us that we come to behave as we feel, when it comes to loving, we come to feel as we behave. Loving persons feel more love. You don't fall in love; you create it and are created by it.

To take pleasure in loving, you must take the time to show good "love manners" by remembering to say "please," "thank you," and "I'm sorry." Too often, we reserve our best manners and common courtesies for strangers while taking our own family and intimate partner for granted.

Wise Loving: Being a pleasant person is as important as being a passionate person

PLEASURE PRESCRIPTION 7.

Just be nice

Research disproves the adage that the good die young. Data shows clearly that, in the race toward an early death, nice guys tend to finish last. When all is said and done, despite all the reams of conflicting, confusing advice from the love manuals, trying to "just be nice" to your lover is the single most important thing you can do in order to love for life. The following pleasure prescription is designed to help you be congenially as well as passionately connected.

Tape-record one of your family or marital meals. As you sit down to dinner, turn on the tape recorder and then forget it's on. About a week later, sit down with your family or spouse and listen to the tape. Count the number of pleasant, good-mannered words during the meal. How many times do you hear "please," "thank you," "well done," "you did a good job," "I really appreciate this," "what a nice thing you did," or common courtesies extended during the meal?

Research has shown that a five-to-one rule applies to being nice. As you count your nice comments, be sure that they outnumber your criticisms and complaints by a ratio of at least five to one. If you are not sure how often you are negative, you are too negative. Increase your niceness ratio significantly.

Being alert for civility and propriety is something we often do with strangers, while we get careless in our manners with those who matter the most.

Virtuous Loving: You can't love yourself unless you first learn to love others

PLEASURE PRESCRIPTION 8.

Love from the outside in

One of the most destructive myths of Western popular psychology is this: "You must love yourself before you love anyone else." The Third Way of Polynesian pleasure teaches, in contrast, that love is a skill learned from the outside in, not from the inside out. Behaving lovingly toward one's parents, siblings, and grandparents is the way one learns to be a lovable and loving person; one does not learn by focusing on loving the self. Our *'ohana* are getting smaller and smaller and more and more estranged, and as a result our love-ability is diminishing. Pleasure Prescription 8 helps you learn to love others as a way of learning to love yourself.

Pick a member of your extended family and commit to reactivating a relationship. Select an aunt or uncle or someone whom you've not maintained a relationship with and start corresponding, sending gifts, calling, and offering to visit and help. Whom might you choose to reach out to? What could you do for that person? (Record your thoughts below.)

_____

_____

_____

_____

_____

_____

_____

_____

Emotionally Intelligent Loving: We are responsible for our own emotions. Never say "you make me" or "now look what you made me do"

PLEASURE PRESCRIPTION 9.

Schedule "Monday support meetings"

No one "makes" us feel anything. We have ultimate control over our own emotions, and we rob ourselves of our pleasure potential when we turn our emotional control over to others. This pleasure prescription is designed to help you be more "affectively accountable."

Monday has been shown to be the most stressful day of the week. Researchers call it "Black Monday" because more sudden deaths occur on Monday mornings than at any other time. Plan for some Monday support meetings at work or at home. At these meetings, take time to find out how others are feeling. Defuse conflicts and discuss problems before the week begins. This is an excellent way to practice emotionally intelligent caring, as you reach out to others and take responsibility for your own emotions as well. Schedule a Monday support meeting, and record your experience below.

Ha'aha'a Aloha (Humble Loving)

We love someone not because he or she is like us but because he or she *is* us. The most powerful of our new sciences, quantum physics, proves that all barriers are illusions. All of us are connected, share the same life energy, and are really one body with billions of brains. Healthy and joyful loving is based on being sensitive to the sameness we share, even when we seem to have many differences.

A corollary to this truth is that loving partners are those who recognize that the goals and needs of a good relationship are those that are held in common, not just those promoted by one partner. Try to make what is important to your loved one important to you as well. Remember that good relationships depend on being—not finding—the right partner.

Wise Loving: Never be sure of yourself

PLEASURE PRESCRIPTION 10.

Practice being *unsure* of yourself

Western culture teaches us to either be sure of ourselves or act as if we are. But pleasurable loving is a matter of tolerantly accepting the flaws in ourselves and those we care about. As Einstein's relativity theory made clear, very little in this world is what it seems to be and nothing is as certain as we wish.

When we are sure of ourselves, we distance ourselves from others because they sense our arrogance and are made uncomfortable by their own feelings of uncertainty, which seem exaggerated by comparison. Work less at being certain of and for yourself and more at the certainty and continuity of the relationship. This tenth pleasure prescription will help you to be much less self-assured.

Make a list of what you consider to be your three greatest strengths in three major areas of life—how you think, how you feel, and how you behave. Next, make a list of your three greatest flaws or weaknesses in these same three areas. Next, meet with someone you love and do this assignment together. This time, list the strengths and weakness of your partner and have her or him do the same for you. Discuss these lists together and you will discover that rational self-confidence takes into account your weaknesses as well as your strengths. You can use the writing space below for your lists.

_____

_____

_____

_____

_____

_____

_____

_____

_____

_____

_____

Virtuous Loving: You have two ears and one mouth. Listen twice as much as you talk

PLEASURE PRESCRIPTION 11.

Avoid ruinous rumors

As you learned in this book and in *The Pleasure Prescription*, ancient Polynesians believed words literally had *mana*. They believed that a joyful life depended on never sending out negative energy—"broadcasting badness"—for fear that it would come crashing back on the sender. This eleventh prescription will help you avoid being hit in your own heart by your negative *mana*.

Resolve to follow one rule in your communication—talk less. Pick one day a week to work really hard on listening rather than talking. Avoid rushing others' speech, finishing their sentences, answering arguments that have not been fully presented, spreading rumors, or gossiping about a person who is not present.

Emotionally Intelligent Loving: Don't let your emotions have you

PLEASURE PRESCRIPTION 12.

Beep for bliss

Our hectic lives can cause us to lose emotional control, to run and "be run" by our emotions. We get so caught up in our work and our busy schedules that our emotions seem to occur as involuntary reflex responses to others' behaviors, not as expressions of our true feelings. Try this prescription to calm down and avoid hyperaffectivity.

Every time the phone rings or your pager beeps, assess your emotional state. Before answering, ask yourself, "How do I feel?" Consider whether your feelings are mere reactions to situations or informed, rational responses. Ask yourself if you are anticipating good or bad news from this call or page. Just being alert to the fact that you are feeling rather than just "doing" will help you regain more control of your emotional life. Try this prescription out today. What happened?

_____

_____

_____

_____

_____

_____

_____

_____

Akahai Aloha (Tender Loving)

Pleasurable loving is as compassionate as it is passionate. Taking quiet time just to be together without talking, doing, making love, worrying, or getting ready to do something else is crucial to joyful loving, as is recognizing and valuing your lover's perspective just as you do your own.

Wise Loving: No one looks at life exactly like you do

PLEASURE PRESCRIPTION 13.

Learn the art of "wish-craft"

In our self-oriented Western world, we often assume that our way is the right way. We miss out on the pleasurable variety and uniqueness of the ways others experience the world. Try this prescription to develop your sense of relative loving.

Make a list of your loved one's three most important life wishes. Think about your lover's or a family member's view of the world and try to identify the three things that they want most from life. How do these wishes compare with your own? Finally and most importantly, consider in what ways you can practice the art of wish-craft to help fulfill the wishes of those who matter most to you. You can record your thoughts in the space below.

Virtuous Loving: Life isn't fair, but people must be

PLEASURE PRESCRIPTION 14.

Pay back your love debts

Most of us have some unpaid emotional debts. We have been lucky and received some benefits in our life that we did not work to get. These are often really gifts from the caring of others. These caring others may be alive now or, as Polynesians believe, they may be ancestors sending their *aloha.*

First, take a pleasure pause. Then write down five of the biggest "breaks" you have received in your life. Consider the real source of these breaks—what role was played by the support and love of others? Next, write down five ways in which you are going to try to repay these love debts back in the future. As with all the assignments in this book, it is the process of taking a pleasure pause and reflecting, not just the lists and words themselves, that is most important in filling this prescription.

_____

_____

_____

_____

_____

_____

_____

_____

_____

_____

_____

_____

Emotionally Intelligent Loving: To feel the energy of love, feel the energy of nature

PLEASURE PRESCRIPTION 15.

Help the earth

Popular psychology stresses the importance of empathy and feeling what other people feel. While you've learned that empathy is indeed an important skill for a pleasurable life, it is equally important to actually *do* something about others' feelings. Empathizing is feeling, but sympathizing is doing. This pleasure prescription helps you discover the joy of sympathy not only for persons but for places and things. This Polynesian pleasure prescription requires you to tune in to and do something to help the *'aina.*

The emotional or *mana* messages from plants, rocks, sand, water, and other natural elements are very subtle, but Polynesians could feel them and you can, too. Sit quietly in an outdoor setting and try to take the essence of a flower or a tree into your soul. Don't just try to see, feel, smell, hear, taste, or use a psychic sense to feel it. Instead, open your heart, activate your seventh sense for healthy pleasure, and try to sense the pleasure it is sending to you. If you try, you will find your love-ability greatly enhanced. Afterward, record what you've experienced.

Chapter Twelve

Aloha Hana (Working with Love): Fifteen Prescriptions for Gratifying Working

Ma ka hana ka'ike
Pronounced "mah kah hah-nah kah ee-kay"

In working, one learns

Can work and pleasure be united? Indeed they can be. Here are fifteen prescriptions—all of them pretested—to bring more pleasure, satisfaction, and meaning to your work.

Ahonui Hana (Patient Working)

Job was a man who endured much suffering. A "job" is often seen as a compensated chore, something one has to do in order to survive or to enjoy other activities—recreation, hobbies, etc. Too often, work and suffering are seen as connected.

Poet Kahlil Gibran said that "work is love made visible." To get pleasure from our work, we must realize that, whether we know it or not, we *are* our work. One of the greatest robbers of the joy of working is the chronic feeling of being too rushed to enjoy what we are doing or to remember why we are doing it. Researcher Suzanne Kobasa Ouellette has found that healthy and hardy working requires a sense of challenge, commitment, and control. These "3 Cs" are the basis for the first three pleasure prescriptions for your work.

Wise Working: Take a little time at work to remember that the ultimate purpose of your work is to make someone else's life easier

PLEASURE PRESCRIPTION 16.

See the challenge

In the space below, write your own job description. In it, emphasize only those factors of your job that meet three criteria: 1) What aspects of your work accomplish positive results for the good of the earth as a whole? 2) Which of the final results of your work make life more pleasurable for other people? 3) Which of your daily activities at work bring you the most pleasure?

Reflecting on the real challenge of your work helps you to keep "getting to it" so that your job does not "get to you."

_____

_____

_____

_____

_____

_____

_____

_____

_____

_____

_____

_____

Virtuous Working: Persistence pays off in pleasure. Don't let the negatives that come with all jobs rob you of the pleasure of working

PLEASURE PRESCRIPTION 17.

Make a job history

List every job you have ever held, all the way back to childhood. List the fun parts of each job and then list the negative aspects of the tasks involved. Compare the joys and hassles of your prior jobs with your current work. You will note that from running a paper route to being president of your own company, every single job had its costs and benefits. You must have much of the patience of Job to do a good job. Resolve to stay *committed* to the ultimate purpose of your work, even if you encounter problems in doing a particular task.

Emotionally Intelligent Working: Accept the fact that your job and the things you work with will "bug" you. Phones, computers, and other high-tech things designed to help can resist and "bite back" at just the wrong times, causing what author Larry Dossey calls a "resistential crisis"

PLEASURE PRESCRIPTION 18.

Know when to give up

Having emotional control at work is essential to your health and happiness and to the joy and well-being of your co-workers. Healthy control does not always mean being in control. It also means having enough emotional wisdom to know when there is very little you can do about a problem. Remember that the leading stressor in work is feeling that you have a lot of responsibility, but very little power. You often cannot do much about your assigned responsibilities, but you *can* empower yourself by knowing when it is time to give up and, as the Polynesians say, just "go with how it goes." Give this prescription a try, and write about your experience below.

Lokahi Hana (Harmonious Working)

Albert Einstein wrote, "If *A* is success in life, then *A* equals *x* plus *y* plus *z*. Work is *x*; *y* is play; and *z* is keeping your mouth shut." As smart as Einstein was, his vision of hard work, hard play, and no communication is a perfect *dis*pleasure prescription. In order to work "softly"—to work with joy—we must learn to enjoying working with others and help them enjoy working with us. Working softly requires communication; it also requires caring about the service your job renders to society and trying to make things less difficult for your co-workers.

Wise Working: Work means different things to different people. Even if people are doing the same tasks, they all view their jobs differently

PLEASURE PRESCRIPTION 19.

Do cross-job interviewing

As often as possible, sit with someone at work whose job is different from yours. If possible, pick someone whose own job may be in danger or someone who has already been laid off. (Whether we are aware of it or not, survivor guilt in the workplace is a strong stressor, so take responsibility for others' problems and help out as much as you can.) Ask your fellow worker how she feels about her job. Be careful not to get caught up in gossip or a "pity party" about how rough things are at work. Just try to learn how someone else feels, try to empathize, and then try to tell your interviewee some of your areas of mutual concern. End the interview with an invitation to talk again. What did you notice during this conversation?

Virtuous Working: Excellence is achieved by working by values rather than for objectives. Hawaiians call this po'okela (pronounced "poh oh-kay-la")

PLEASURE PRESCRIPTION 20.

Value your values

Take time to identify the one value in your working life that is not negotiable or subject to compromise, the one value that you will never surrender even if it means financial loss. There may be many work values that are important to you, but decide on one. Write it on a poster or card to keep in clear sight when you are working, and then use the space below to write about why this value is essential to you.

_____

_____

_____

_____

_____

_____

_____

_____

_____

_____

_____

_____

_____

Emotionally Intelligent Working: Your work is a part of your life. Always bring your work problems home

PLEASURE PRESCRIPTION 21.

Make a "work review" appointment

It is impossible to separate work from our home life, so it is a good idea to set a separate and limited time to discuss work issues with your family. Talk with your family, pick a "work review" time convenient for everyone (remember, school counts as work), and write the time below. This time should not be before or during dinner, but after dinner can be a very good time. Don't do anything else but talk about each family member's work life. Don't do the dishes or watch television while doing your work review with your family. Record what happens in the space below.

'Olu'olu Hana (Pleasant Working)

Watch out for the "Sisyphus Syndrome" I described earlier, the joyless, repetitive striving that leads only to fatigue and depression. When work begins to feel like we are pushing the same old stone up the same hill day after day, only to have it roll back down again, all the pleasantness goes out of work and out of you. The next three pleasure prescriptions are designed to help you stay pleasant in the workplace.

Wise Working: Don't just "get the job done." Think about new ways, no matter how small, to put pleasure and variety into your work

PLEASURE PRESCRIPTION 22.

Make a "wondering about work" list

Below, write down three ways that you could do your job differently and still get done what you have to do. Consider anything that might be allowed where you work, such as playing different music every day, changing your time of arrival or departure, or working on the weekend and taking a day off during the week. Ask yourself what it is that might make your work an avocation instead of a vocation.

_____

_____

_____

_____

_____

_____

_____

_____

_____

_____

_____

_____

_____

_____

Virtuous Working: Always do less than you can do. Avoid working in spurts in order to buy time to rest

PLEASURE PRESCRIPTION 23.

Try pleasurable pacing

If you are doing all you can do, you are working at the edge of your physical and psychological limit. The average span of very efficient focus on any task is not much more than thirty minutes. After that, efficiency falls drastically. Break your job into as many small segments as possible and take pleasure pauses or some SAFE time between your more intense work periods. You can use the space below to record a pleasurable-pacing plan.

Emotionally Intelligent Working: Don't express your anger at work. Even if you are in the right, anger will always come back to haunt you

PLEASURE PRESCRIPTION 24.

Don't "let it all out." Write it all out

Research shows that the act of writing out your anger rather than verbalizing it can help slow and calm you down. Keep a log of your anger at work. When you reread entries, look for the following three places to intervene against the damaging effects of anger. 1) Identify the thoughts you have about people and life that seem to "set you off." Remember that you can't really change people, but you can change how you think about people. 2) Write down the feelings that follow such thoughts. The thoughts that start an aggression cycle are usually cynical, and feelings of anger come from thinking cynically. 3) Describe how you show your anger. Are you slamming doors, swearing, or spreading rumors at work? Keep these three interventions against anger and aggression in mind and you will be better able to avoid the aggressive acts that always end up turning back against you. You can begin your log here.

_____

_____

_____

_____

_____

Ha'aha'a Hana (Humble Working)

You can't "do it all yourself." Dr. Sherman A. James at the University of Michigan has identified what he calls John Henryism, a personality pattern characterized by joyless working, work stress, and, as a result, poor health. It is named for the American folk hero who tried to outperform a steam-powered drill using only a hammer and a handheld tool. John Henry fell dead upon completion of his task. He had proved his point, but at a fatal cost.

Wise working: Don't be so certain that you can do anything, if only you set your mind to it

PLEASURE PRESCRIPTION 25.

Make a "can't do" list

While popular psychology stresses a "can-do" orientation to working and living, a life of healthy pleasure requires that we acknowledge that there are things we just cannot do, no matter how badly we want to or how hard we try. Remember this pleasure principle: If you want to do something very, very badly, that is usually how you will do it. Take a pleasure pause and list things you just cannot or will not do.

_____

_____

_____

_____

_____

_____

_____

_____

_____

_____

_____

_____

_____

Virtuous Working: Be clear on your limits

PLEASURE PRESCRIPTION 26.

Just say "maybe"

Contrary to the currently popular "just do it" and "just say no" approaches, healthy pleasure requires that you learn and respect your limits by saying and meaning "maybe." Take an index card and write the words JUST SAY "MAYBE" on it in large letters. Keep that card near your phone as a reminder to beware of committing yourself to tasks that will end up making you busier than you already are or making you feel guilty for not coming through. What other "just say maybe" ideas can you think of to help simplify and calm your life? You can record some ideas below.

Emotionally Intelligent Working: Smell the smoke before you burn out

PLEASURE PRESCRIPTION 27.

Check for burnout

Prevent burnout by being alert to very first signs that you are catching fire. Keep this Ten-Item Work Tenseness List near you at work. Review the list whenever you're starting to feel stressed. If you score three or more points, take a pleasure pause for some SAFE time.

THE TEN-ITEM WORK TENSENESS LIST

1. _____ Am I making silly, stupid mistakes that I usually don't make?

2. _____ Am I having work stress symptoms, such as headaches, backaches, or bowel or stomach symptoms?

3. _____ Am I starting to feel angry and short-tempered?

4. _____ Am I feeling sleepy?

5. _____ Am I feeling resentful that I'm doing more than I should or more than I'm paid to do?

6. _____ Am I feeling that I have too many responsibilities for the amount of power I have?

7. _____ Am I feeling that others are just not doing their share?

8. _____ Am I getting sarcastic?

9. _____ Am I threatening to quit?

10. _____ Am I taking my anger out on machines?

Akahai Hana (Gentle Working)

Historically, connections between work and suffering have been taken for granted. Recently, people have been trying to make their work a more joyful part of life. Working gently and joyfully is now more of an objective than is hard work, suffering, or searching for joy only outside the workplace. People are trying to unite their avocations and vocations "just as their two eyes make one sight," as poet Robert Frost wrote in "Two Tramps in Mud Time." Working gently is crucial to working joyfully.

Wise Working: Be soft-coasting, not hard-driving

PLEASURE PRESCRIPTION 28.

Check for "job jaw"

When you start to feel tense at work, place a soft wooden pencil between your teeth while doing your job. In a few minutes, check it for teeth marks. When you end up with a job-chewed pencil, you are likely developing job jaw. Work stress is conveyed not only to your jaw but to your whole body. Put what one of my patients calls her "pressure-pitted pencil" someplace at work where it will remind you to loosen up!

Virtuous Working: Don't just "do your job"

PLEASURE PRESCRIPTION 29.

Help out as much as you work out

The honorable way of working is to feel that your job is not done as long as someone else is still working. At a time when we are more and more isolated from one another at work, medical research is showing that communing with others is good for our health. Take as much time during your work day as you can to help someone do his or her job. Trade off jobs when possible and, instead of seeing your job as "yours," see working as something "we" do. You will derive great pleasure from coming in a little early or leaving work a little later if you use that extra time to help a fellow worker get more done.

Emotionally Intelligent Working: Face it. You are emotionally involved in your work

PLEASURE PRESCRIPTION 30.

Be emotionally ready to work

You are emotionally involved in your work, so keep a work diary that tracks your emotional ups and downs during the work day. You will find through keeping this diary that there are times during the day when you are really "up" for working and other times when emotional downs or distractions make you much less efficient. Pick the emotionally up times to do the difficult jobs. You might record some of your first entries in the space below.

_____

_____

_____

_____

_____

_____

_____

_____

_____

_____

_____

_____

_____

_____

Chapter Thirteen

Aloha Pa'ani (Loving Playing):
Fifteen Prescriptions for Hearty Playing

He 'olina leo ka ke aloha
Pronounced slowly as "hey oh-lean-ah lay-oh ka kay ah-lo-ha"

Joyousness is in the voice of love

Play, in most people's minds, equals pleasure. But how much pleasure do we actually get from our play? Too often, we turn play into competitive, hard-driving sport or we segregate play from the rest of life, thinking of it as something we do only on weekends or during vacations. Here's the antidote: fifteen powerful prescriptions for more joyous, relaxed, and truly pleasure-producing play.

Ahonui Pa'ani (Patient Playing)

Play is process-oriented, while productivity is goal-oriented. Healthy play requires that you remember that results will not matter if we really love what we are doing for its own sake.

Play has been defined by researchers as an activity that is out of the ordinary, not serious, expresses freedom, and results in total immersion and involvement of the individual. Play is getting completely lost in what you are doing and being free of thoughts of "getting back to real life." Play is the purest expression of healthy pleasure, but much of the joy and healthy benefits of play are diminished by the hurried ways we try to crowd recreation into our stress-filled daily life. Healthy pleasure requires that you have the patience to take plenty of time to play and that you make play a regular part of your life, not just a temporary escape.

Wise Playing: You don't have to "do anything" to play. Take time for playful thoughts

PLEASURE PRESCRIPTION 31.

Mentally mess around

Write down as many weird, odd, peculiar, unorthodox, and unconventional phrases as you can imagine. Don't censor yourself; just start writing. To help you, here are some starters for mentally messing around.

1. If cars could fly, I'd . . .

_____

2. If men had babies, men would learn to . . .

_____

_____

3. If sex was allowed only one night a year, people would . . .

_____

_____

4. If I looked like I usually feel, I'd look just like . . .

_____

_____

5. If men married men and women married women, marriage would . .

_____

_____

Now think up some of your own ideas for mentally messing around.

Virtuous Playing: Pleasurable playing requires celebrating losing

PLEASURE PRESCRIPTION 32.

Be a trickster

Hawaiian myths and the myths of many other indigenous peoples are based on fun and tricks. The next time you play tennis, golf, or any other competitive sport, try to gently trick your opponent into believing he or she has won. Make it a close contest and then lose without letting your opponent know that you've lost intentionally. It will require some practice, but you can learn to be a very happy loser and to take great pleasure from the pride you have helped your opponent to feel. Don't ruin this prescription by ever telling your opponent what you have done. This prescription is intended to be pleasing prank, not a mean manipulation. After you have tried being a trickster, write below some notes on how it made you feel and list other ways you might be able to be a gentle trickster.

_____

_____

_____

_____

_____

_____

_____

_____

_____

_____

_____

_____

_____

_____

Emotionally Intelligent Playing: Playing is, by its very nature, intended to be fun. Don't take the fun out of playing

PLEASURE PRESCRIPTION 33.

Don't take play too seriously

We often ruin the benefits of joyful play by becoming angry or impatient with ourselves when we don't do our best. Take a pleasure pause and write down the times you can remember that you ruined your own fun or others' enjoyment by getting angry while playing. Keep your list handy to check before you play again.

_____

_____

_____

_____

_____

_____

_____

_____

_____

_____

Lokahi Pa'ani (Harmonious Playing)

Too often, play has come to mean competition. Healthy, joyful play is based on cooperation and sharing, volleying a ball back and forth rather than trying to always win the point. If one plays to win, one is always either failing at their play or playing with someone whom they have helped to feel like a loser.

Wise Playing: With the advent of computer games (which are usually played solo rather than in groups) and Western society's growing emphasis on competition and individual excellence, the joy and the health benefits of shared play are diminishing. Learn anew the "old" forms of play and rediscover their gifts

PLEASURE PRESCRIPTION 34.

Board games aren't boring

Get out your old board games. Spend some TV- and computer-free nights, get together as a family, play as teams, and enjoy the older, simpler games such as Monopoly, Scrabble, Clue, or various card games. Unless we ruin them through competitiveness, board and card games are by their nature slower, quieter, and less intense than electronic games. They require and teach more cooperation, mutual involvement, and planning. What did you notice during your board games? Write about the games below.

_____

_____

_____

_____

_____

_____

_____

_____

_____

_____

_____

_____

Virtuous Playing: Healthy play is shared play. Proudly show that you enjoy sharing play

PLEASURE PRESCRIPTION 35.

Create your own family art gallery

Parents often display their children's pictures. Take some pleasure pauses to do some drawings and murals as a family. Display everyone's work. Dedicate one wall in your kitchen or basement to regular displays of family painting and writing.

Emotionally Intelligent Playing: Don't be yourself, lose yourself in your playing

PLEASURE PRESCRIPTION 36.

Play by playing roles

Experiment with different roles. One of the greatest advantages of healthy play is that you can safely experiment with activities that you would never otherwise try. If you usually lead, play games where you must follow. Be a team player, not the captain. If you are a real go-getter, play games in which you back off and allow others to do the going and getting. You can record your experiences—which will probably surprise you and even delight you—in the space below.

'Olu'olu Pa'ani (Pleasant Playing)

While we often think of play as purely relaxing, it is actually a process of seeking out challenges, experimenting, and enjoying pressure-free, congenial, spontaneous activities that don't hurt anyone. Always remember, "it's only a game."

Wise Playing: If you always play to win, you are making a lot of people losers

PLEASURE PRESCRIPTION 37.

Stop making life a contest

Take a pleasure pause and ask yourself this question: "Is my life a series of contests?" (You can write your answer in the space below.) Even our games can seem like "mini-wars" that lead to feelings of subtle resentment when we lose. Our days do not have to be endless series of contests, beginning with the starting gun of the alarm clock and ending with a surrender to sleep. Make your life a series of celebrations rather than a series of contests.

Virtuous Playing: Don't just have fun for yourself, make fun of yourself

PLEASURE PRESCRIPTION 38.

Create a daily stupid headline

At the end of the day, sit with your family or fellow workers and write brief, exaggerated, silly headlines that describe your day. "Man found dead at the end of his deadline," was one example from an executive. His wife's headline was, "Woman got everything done. Died anyway." Make fun of your stressed life. Try some stupid headlines together here.

_____

_____

_____

_____

_____

_____

_____

_____

_____

_____

_____

_____

_____

_____

_____

_____

_____

_____

Emotionally Intelligent Playing: If you're getting angry when you play, play at being angry

PLEASURE PRESCRIPTION 39.

Enlist a surrogate sulker

Many of us can be very bad sports and bring our stress and competitiveness to our games. Have somebody in your family show you how you show your anger. Have them act out how you look losing at an activity you value. What did you learn?

_____

_____

_____

_____

_____

_____

_____

_____

_____

_____

_____

Ha'aha'a Pa'ani (Humble Playing)

Much of modern playing has lost the sense of "team." Even when two teams compete, there always seems to be a "star" who outshines all the other players. Humble playing means not getting in someone's face, gloating, showing off, spiking the ball, or dancing in the end zone. When you show off, you shut others out, and the joy of the game is gone for them.

Wise Playing: We live in a society that is results-oriented. But wise playing requires pleasure-oriented games

PLEASURE PRESCRIPTION 40.

Don't keep score

Golf, play tennis, play cards, or play any game you enjoy, but totally forget about scoring. Scoring means comparing skills, but healthy playing means playing even if you aren't comparatively skillful.

Virtuous Playing: One of the best things that can be said about you is that you are a lot of fun to play with.

PLEASURE PRESCRIPTION 41.

Would you want to play with you?

Take a pleasure pause and reflect on this question. (You can record your answer in the space below.) If the answer is "no" or "sometimes," lighten up! Remember your parents' admonition: "Play nice!"

_____

_____

_____

_____

_____

_____

_____

_____

_____

Emotionally Intelligent Playing: Dostoevsky wrote that, if you really want to get to know a person, you should watch that person laugh. If the person laughs well, deeply, and sincerely, she is sure to be a good person. Laughter is the announcement that you have filled a pleasure prescription

PLEASURE PRESCRIPTION 42.

Laugh hard, even if you don't feel like it

Researchers know that when you smile, your body reacts in a very healthy way and telegraphs the joy of that smile to every cell in your body. The same is true of laughter. Find a partner who is in need of some pleasure and follow this "chuckle-robics" list together.

1. First, smirk. Curl the outer corners of your mouth upward.

2. Next, smile. Squint your eyes and bare your teeth. Fake it if you have to. Smile hard.

3. Snicker. This is the first sound release of your chuckle-robics.

4. Chuckle. Give off slow, gentle barking sounds.

5. Giggle. Bark in a higher-pitched voice, and then bark faster.

6. Laugh. Tilt your head back, close your eyes, and go from a bark to a yap.

7. Guffaw. Yap faster and hit your thighs with your hands.

8. Howl. Say out loud, "I really kill me" (meaning that you've completely lost awareness of yourself). Prolong your yaps into long yelps, and roll on the floor.

Note: If you notice that fluid is seeping from your eyes (or other places), don't worry! You are just having a little laughter leakage that is draining your misery. Laughter leakage means that you are doing very intense and beneficial chuckle-robics.

Akahai Paʻanai (Tender Playing)

"Work hard, play hard" is a very popular phrase, but it is the wrong way to live a long, joyful life. Work joyfully and play gently.

Wise Playing: Your Western brain takes life very seriously. Teach it to lighten up and enjoy life

PLEASURE PRESCRIPTION 43.

Treat your psychosclerosis (hardening of the attitudes)

Take some pleasure pauses to watch funny videos and read humorous books. Consult Glenn C. Ellenbogen's *Directory of Humor Magazines and Humor Organizations in America* (New York: Wry-Bred Press, 1985). Visit the humor section in your bookstore. See John Cassidy and B.C. Rimbeauz's *Juggling for the Complete Klutz* (Palo Alto, CA: Klutz Press, 1988), and learn to be a bad juggler! Aphorist G. K. Chesterton described true play when he said, "If a thing is worth doing at all, it is worth doing badly." Another way to treat your psychosclerosis is to participate in non-competitive games. A good resource for games like this is Matt Weinstein's and Joel Goodman's *Everybody's Guide to Non-Competitive Play* (San Luis Obispo, CA: Impact Publishing, 1988). Make a list below of other resources that would help you take more pleasure pauses in your life.

_____

_____

_____

_____

_____

_____

_____

_____

_____

_____

Virtuous Playing: Creative humorist Loretta LaRoche says that good humor is the ability to feel joy, peace, and harmony within yourself and in your surroundings. She states that it is never too late to have a happy childhood, if we will take time for some healthy regression. She warns that life is not a dress rehearsal and that we are giving a great gift to the world by sharing good humor

PLEASURE PRESCRIPTION 44.

Do your best to stop global whining

Take several pleasure pauses a day to think in silly, irreverent, iconoclastic ways about what you can do to cheer up the world's grouches. Send the office grump a bouquet of flowers or a very kind card. Don't sign it, just sit back, watch what happens, and enjoy the act of giving pleasure to someone who can be a real pain. (You can record other ideas below.)

Emotionally Intelligent Playing: Anger quickly overwhelms good humor. When we are cynical, we will eventually become angry. When we feel anger, we will eventually become aggressive. When we feel trust, we will eventually become joyful. When we feel joy, we will eventually show loving tenderness

PLEASURE PRESCRIPTION 45.

Create more pleasurable profanity

In the space provided below, make a list of the profanities you use most often. Beside each profanity, write the name of a nongenital and non-rectal body part, such as "elbow," "foot," "knee," or "nose." When you are letting yourself get angry at someone, think of that body part instead of saying the old profanity. Remember that no matter how tough life gets, it is always possible to be your own entertainment center.

Chapter Fourteen

Aloha Lapa'au (Healing Love): Fifteen Pleasure Prescriptions for Jubilant Healing

Ua ola loka i ke aloha
Pronounced "oo-ah oh-lah low-kah ee kay ah-lo-ha"

Love gives mental and physical health

If your pain and suffering are very hot and immediate, you probably don't want to wait to take the fifteen pleasure prescriptions for healing. Here are some 2,000-year-old, pretested healing rituals you can use for some emotional first aid before moving on to the pleasure prescriptions.

There are two key pleasurable Polynesian ways to heal at times of intense life challenge—restorative grace and re-energizing grit.

Grace is the warmth of *aloha* achieved by restoring balance and connection with life, family, and the earth. Rather than using a mind-over-body approach and seeking to instantly solve our problems and muffle our pain, grace urges us, even at the coldest times, to rediscover the healing warmth of loving connection with *Akua* (God), our *'ohana,* and the *'aina.*

No matter how hopeless and stressful life seems to you right now, take a pleasure pause and begin practicing your pleasure prescriptions for the tough times of life by saying over and over again this ancient Hawaiian chant, designed to summon forth the restorative warmth of the sacred breath of life:

Ka la i ka mauli ola.
Pronounced "ka la ee ka mah-oo-lee oh-la"
The sun is the source of life.

Chanting for the grace of healing warmth starts the healing process. It helps you catch your breath when you feel as if the breath has been completely knocked out of you.

You can also chant for grit, or the strength to grow and become whole and connected again. Read the following ancient Hawaiian chant.

He 'a'ali'i ku makani mai au.
Pronounced "hey ah ah-lee ee koo ma-kah-nee ma-ee ow"
I am a wind-resisting *'a'ali'i* [a strong bush that withstands the worst of winds. It twists and bends but seldom breaks].

Take some pleasure pauses and repeat this chant over and over again, and then alternate the two chants. Write a bit about how this chanting makes you feel.

_____

_____

_____

_____

_____

Now, here are fifteen pleasure prescriptions for life's worst times.

Ahonui Lapa'au (Patient Healing)

You can't rush healing. Remember the first of the Buddha's Four Noble Truths: "Life is suffering." Healing through a severe illness and healthy grieving through a terrible loss are assisted when we fully and deeply accept the fact that life is as difficult as it is wonderful.

Wise Healing: Things are never black or white. Take a few pleasure pauses to remember and share the good times with someone, even as you struggle to make it through the bad times

PLEASURE PRESCRIPTION 46.

Remember the good times

Take a pleasure pause and, in the space below, write down one of the times in your life when you felt the happiest, strongest, and healthiest. Read the description out loud. Doing so won't make the bad times go away, but it will allow some of the stored joy of past good times to provide a little energy to help you make it through your challenges. Play some Hawaiian music to help you focus on the joy of life.

_____

_____

_____

_____

_____

_____

_____

_____

_____

_____

_____

_____

_____

Virtuous Healing: One of the best ways to heal is to try to heal others. When you are sick, start giving. Don't just be a receiver. As unlikely as it may seem, many people become angry with those in pain. They may imagine that someone who suffers also adopts a "victim" or "poor me" attitude. To counteract this defensive rejection, keep giving support even when you need it the most

PLEASURE PRESCRIPTION 47.

Send flowers *from* the hospital

When you are very sick or feeling very low, send flowers, make a call, or reach out and help someone else. One of the greatest dangers to healing is being stuck in "receiver mode" and thus losing the benefits of altruistic behavior. Below, record other ideas for helping others when you're feeling down.

_____

_____

_____

_____

_____

_____

_____

_____

_____

_____

_____

_____

_____

_____

_____

Emotionally Intelligent Healing: Facts are facts, but implications are choices

PLEASURE PRESCRIPTION 48.

Do some "denial distractions" and practice rational denial

Denial of facts can be dangerous to your health and healing, but compliantly accepting imposed implications and consequences of those facts limits your healing capacity and creativity. For example, you shouldn't deny that you've broken your leg. But you can deny that breaking a leg forbids you to lead an active, loving life. And you can deny, at least for a time, the physical pain and struggle of healing from your injury.

If you are suffering a life challenge now, remember that you do not have to tough it out all of the time. Distract yourself, get away from your problem as much as you can, and deny that the problem exists for just a few minutes. This little denial distraction allows for a spurt of badly needed energy that helps you to go back and deal with your situation. Write down some denial distractions that would be helpful in your life.

Lokahi Lpa'au (Harmonious Healing)

The Polynesian pleasure approach to dealing with the tough times of life stresses that self-healing is a myth. Healing requires achieving harmony with others and restoring balance, not a one-mind-over-one-body approach.

Wise Healing: When crisis strikes, never say, "Now look what has happened to me." Say, "Now look what we are going through together"

"Draw" your attention to your disconnection

Draw your problem in the space below. No matter how silly it seems, draw what your crisis, loss, illness, or conflict looks like. Make sure that your drawing is full of other people, places, animals, flowers, and objects. Make sure that you are not just drawing your suffering or problem.

Now study your drawing and look for signs of disconnection. What is missing from your drawing? What person, place, or thing added to your drawing would make it a happier, healthier drawing? How can you connect in your mind or heart with whatever is missing?

Virtuous Healing: Crises tend to turn inward. But reaching outward is our greatest need in times of pain, sorrow, or illness

PLEASURE PRESCRIPTION 50.

Hurry up and reach out

When things seem very, very bad, take a pleasure pause and do something very, very nice for a complete stranger. Give money to a homeless person, do a little volunteer work (even if you feel very tired and stressed), or help a needy person in any way you can. Just be sure you reach out and help a complete stranger. This "donational healing" pays big dividends in healing. Below, you can record other ideas for reaching out.

_____

_____

_____

_____

_____

_____

_____

_____

_____

_____

_____

_____

_____

_____

_____

Emotionally Intelligent Healing: Don't miss the lessons of suffering. Severe challenges help us to learn and grow more than do our lucky breaks

PLEASURE PRESCRIPTION 51.

Look on the dark side

Even though you may have been told to "look on the bright side," a little productive pessimism can be a very healing thing. Take a pleasure pause and remember that the pleasure you learned about in this book and *The Pleasure Prescription* is not constant happiness, but complete immersion in all that life offers us.

When you are facing conflict or pain, spend some SAFE (sit and feel everything) time and totally experience every one of your emotions. Record your feelings in the space below. Ask yourself how your body feels and what your heart senses as you go through the dark side of life. Remember that the light side of life that always follows pain will be brighter for your awareness and learning during your trip through the shadows.

_____

_____

_____

_____

_____

'Olu'olu Lapa'au (Pleasant Healing)

You need people to help you heal. Healing means getting better by becoming connected and whole again; it doesn't necessarily mean curing or solving your illness or problem. Being whole means trying to stay connected with others and the world. View every one of your personal crises as a cry for more personal connection, and remember that pleasantness is essential to forging and preserving connections during bad times—just as it is during good times.

Wise Healing: Tough times can make difficult people. When we suffer terribly, we can become unpleasant and drive people away just when we need them most. Being angry about our situation is a natural reaction to the random and seemingly unfair nature of the chaos of life, but confessing anger to yourself rather than expressing it is the pleasurable way to live during your crises

PLEASURE PRESCRIPTION 52.

Confess your anger

All life crises carry the seeds of anger and resentment toward some person or some event. In the space below, write down a few sentences about why you are angry with your problem. Write down your anger and then, with vigor, cross out every line of your sentences so that they cannot be seen.

_____

_____

_____

_____

_____

_____

_____

_____

_____

_____

_____

_____

_____

Virtuous Healing: When things get bad, work out. It is crucial that you stay in the best physical shape and maintain as much stamina as you can, even when many things are going wrong or you are feeling so weak that you can hardly move. Remember that exercise drains stress and anger as it builds strength, and thus contributes to your ability to maintain pleasant relationships in bad times

PLEASURE PRESCRIPTION 53.

Don't let up when you're down

If you are in a hospital bed, move your arms and legs to some of your Hawaiian music. You might even try to *kaholo* or move to and fro in any way you can to the rhythms from paradise. If you are feeling very down over a severe loss, get up and go for a run or as brisk a walk as you can manage.

Even if you cannot keep your mind off your problems, give your body a chance to contribute some energy of its own to your healing process. Keep the body moving and remember that healing through the tough times is not just "mind over body" but also "body over mind." Try drawing or doodling in the space below something that will make you smile.

Emotionally Intelligent Healing: Go ahead and feel sorry for yourself. No matter how much you have heard about staying strong through it all, go ahead and feel badly, cry, get angry, and ask "Why me?" Doing so will enable you to keep 'olu'olu (pleasantness) in your interactions with others, as your self-pity will find out outlets

PLEASURE PRESCRIPTION 54.

Throw your own "pity party" and loosen your upper lip

Healing is reestablishing balance and connection. Healthy balance is not just being up, staying strong, and having a stiff upper lip; it also means making space for less pleasant emotions. Set a timer for ten minutes and have a short pity party for yourself. Be sure the party ends when the buzzer goes off and reassure yourself that you can throw a pity party again when you need one.

First, take a pleasure pause. Then go ahead and feel very sorry for yourself. Intentionally pout your lower lip. Look sad for your full ten minutes, and then put on a happier face when your timer goes off, even if you have to fake it. Just smiling will cause a little positive emotional spurt. You might write about your pity party in the space below.

_____

_____

_____

_____

_____

Ha'aha'a Lapa'au (Humble Healing)

Time does not heal all wounds. Sometimes it is darkest just before it gets darker. None of us get our way. We all get "the way."

The wholeness of healing sometimes requires that we give up some control and just go with the flow and let others take care of us. A little healthy codependence can go a long way toward helping us heal.

Wise Healing: Life is fair, but our earthly perspective on fairness is very narrow. We need a sacred perspective as well

PLEASURE PRESCRIPTION 55.

Practice the five-prayer minimum

There is no longer any doubt about it. Prayer heals. Modern research is proving what every religion has always known. See the table below for more information on what prayer can do for your life.

The Benefits of Faith

Western scientists seem amazed and puzzled by the power of prayer. Here are just a few of the findings about spirituality that are creating pause—and prayer—among Western physicians:

Among 232 elderly patients undergoing open-heart surgery, those who were deeply religious were more likely to survive the surgery.

Eleven of twelve studies showed that religious commitment is associated with curtailed drug use.

Heavy smokers who attend church regularly are four times less likely to have high blood pressure than smokers who do not go to church, prompting one scientist to say, "If you are going to smoke, take your butt to a church."

A survey of 91,909 persons who had attended church regularly showed that they had 50 percent fewer deaths from coronary artery disease, 56 percent fewer deaths from emphysema, 74 percent fewer deaths from cirrhosis, and 53 percent fewer surgeries.

A study showed that patients receiving heart bypass surgery who were prayed for had fewer complications than those who were not prayed for.

These findings show that something very powerful takes place in the realm of the spiritual. How is the spiritual affecting and inspiring your life today? The warning label for the pleasure prescription reads, "Take only as directed by your soul and never without living the blissful spiritual life that gives this prescription its power."

—from *The Pleasure Prescription*

In the space on the following page, write your own prayer of healing. Take several pleasure pauses during consecutive days and really work on your prayer. Write it over and over, and say it out loud many times before you decide on its final form—don't be afraid to try many sorts of prayers until you find the one that feels right. Based on what Ho'ala Hou and other research organizations have learned about prayers that seem to work, here are some "prayer pointers" for your writing.

1. Make it brief. Create something that you can say over and over, anywhere, any time.

2. Relate your words to the natural world around you—the flowers, trees, and streams.

3. Don't tell God what to do. Instead, ask God to work His or Her will in your life.

4. Don't pray for yourself. Pray for everyone, everywhere.

5. Include the name of past ancestors as a means of bringing the love of the past into the present healing.

6. Repeat your prayer five times every time you pray. This will cause you to slow down and concentrate on your praying. You don't always have to say your prayers out loud.

7. Don't just "send" your prayers. Open your heart and listen. All prayers are answered, but we often do not listen with our heart and soul, and thus we may never hear or understand the answers.

Here's my own example of a prayer. I used it during chemotherapy, radiation, and a bone-marrow transplant while I was recovering from cancer.

"Dear Lord, please be with my wife, Celest; my sons, Roger and Scott; my grandmother, Lita; my father, Frank; and with my mother, Carol. Please work Your divine will for all of us at our time of suffering, and for the trees in our yard, the flowers near our pond, and my dog, Hana, and all animals who suffer. Dear Lord, please hear that I'm listening."

Now write your own prayer in the space below.

Virtuous Healing: What goes around comes around, so keep sending positive aloha *to those around you even when you are very, very down*

PLEASURE PRESCRIPTION 56.

Stay accessible when you're vulnerable

When we suffer, we often lower our tolerance threshold. We become curt, cynical, or envious of those who are not suffering, or we try to be "clever" enough to outsmart our problems. Remember that *ha'aha'a la-pa'aua* (humble healing) requires that you abandon cynicism and cleverness and humbly open your heart. As the main character in the play *Harvey* said, near its end, "I've tried being clever and I've tried being pleasant. I prefer being pleasant."

Work hard to be a pleasant patient and to maintain a gentle, caring style. Don't be complacent, compliant, or surrendering, but do be docile. One of the meanings of the word *docile* is "easily teachable," and people send us lessons more easily when we are kind and considerate, even when we don't feel much like being nice to anyone. No one can teach a stubborn, rude, angry student. Remember, healing is a matter of learning. Write down below the person in your life who you considered your best teacher and what it was that made you open to your teacher.

_____

_____

_____

_____

_____

_____

_____

_____

_____

Emotionally Intelligent Healing: Your beliefs can become your biology. Even though you are very emotional in times of crisis, you don't have to surrender emotional control to that crisis

PLEASURE PRESCRIPTION 57.

Good grieving

All life problems involve some form of loss—loss of control, loss of a loved one, loss of health, or loss of a job. In the space below, write down what you have lost in your crisis. If you have lost a person, write down what you have lost by that person's death or departure. Remember when you read what you have written that the good and cherished things you have "lost" are not really gone. These things can never be erased. Like all events in the cosmos, once they have happened, they just are, and they are forever available to your loving recall.

Akahai Lapau (Tender Healing)

The West focuses on doing much more than on being. During tough times, we often try to *do* our way through problems, rather than considering our problems as invitations to enter into a new, gentler way of being.

_____

_____

_____

_____

_____

_____

_____

_____

_____

_____

The last three of the sixty pleasure prescriptions are presented in the form of contemplative affirmations. They are quotes from three *kahuna* from Hawai'i. I suggest you take a long pleasure pause, put on some of your Hawaiian music, find a very quiet and pleasure-friendly place, sit down with someone close to you who is willing to learn to write pleasure prescriptions, and together read these last three prescriptions aloud.

PLEASURE PRESCRIPTION 58.

On the wisdom of tender healing

A *kahuna* from the island of Kaua'i: "Our worst problems are divine windows to inspiration—an opportunity to 'in-spire' and breathe in more deeply the lessons sent from our ancestors. They are not punishments, but they are gentle, subtle, sublime retributional lessons. They are invitations to greater and deeper connection with *Akua, 'ohana,* and the *'aina.* If we will learn, we will heal."

PLEASURE PRESCRIPTION 59.

On the virtue of tender healing

A *kahuna* from the Big Island of Hawai'i: "Those who are given great suffering are given the chance to be our greatest *kumu* [teachers]. They have been to a side of life that all of us will visit and they have felt what all of us will feel. From their torture can come great tenderness. Sufferers are our navigators, exploring for us, if we will learn with them, the ways to ride the troubled seas that we all must eventually sail."

PLEASURE PRESCRIPTION 60.

On the emotional intelligence of tender healing

A *kahuna* from my home island of Maui: "One cannot heal when one is angry. One can only heal if one is willing to look, without self-blame or other-blame, at where they have disconnected. 'Why me?' is a question that does not promote healing, but answering 'Where should I reconnect?' is the path to being whole again and returning to balance. Balance and connection are the paths to a healthy, pleasing, and pleased life."

Chapter Fifteen

How to Be Your Own Pleasure Pharmacologist

"Paradise is where I am."
VOLTAIRE

You are living in paradise. Learning to write your own pleasure pre-scriptions is similar to prescribing medication for a child or adult with attention deficit disorder. Each prescription should help you focus on paradise—upon the wondrous fact of being alive—and teach you ways to share that pleasure with others. Each prescription should help you past the hyperactivity, agitation, and loneliness that prevent you from reveling in the simple joys that are obvious to those who, like many Polynesians, are able to pay attention to their place in paradise.

As I pointed out in the preface to this book, you don't have to move to Hawai'i to find healthy pleasure, because you are creating your own heaven and hell right this moment, right where you are. Paradise is not a place and a life of shared pleasure is not a goal; both are ways of living day-to-day and ways of sharing the sacred gift of life. This chapter sum-marizes what you have read in this book by presenting six steps—a pleasure-prescription writer's manual—for writing your own pleasure prescriptions.

STEP 1.

Make a pleasure pad

Unlike real pharmacists, who fill written prescriptions written by physicians, you have to be both the prescriber and filler of your pleasure prescriptions. To do so, you will need to make your own pleasure prescription pad. You can use a small notebook that fits easily into your pocket and is sturdy enough to take a lot of use.

On each of five pages of your pleasure pad, write the names of the weekdays in a one-week period. Write the date by each day. Include only Monday through Friday, and then pick a sixth page to title either Saturday or Sunday. This will be your "*aloha* review" day. (You can leave the week's seventh day off the pleasure pad altogether.)

That sixth day is the day of the week that you will set aside to allow the behavioral and physical changes that come from learning a more balanced, pleasure-filled life to sink in. Just as many of the benefits from exercise are felt during the days on which you don't work out, spending one day a week letting the neurohormonal effects of pleasure prescriptions take hold is a good way to get your body and mind used to a more pleasurable life.

On this sixth page, record any comments and feelings you may have on your *aloha* review day—a kind of periodic delight diary. Make a brief delight-diary entry on each sixth day or have someone very close to you review your pleasure pad and make an entry for you.

Now, return to your Monday to Friday pages. Write the phrases below on each of five weekday pages of your pleasure pad. Leave plenty of space between each phrase.

Persistently patient

Harmoniously united

Pleasantly agreeable

Modestly humble

Tenderly gentle

Pleasure prescription for today:

Now that you have your pleasure pad prepared, keep it with you wherever you go. Consider it every bit as important as your day planner, cellular phone, or pager. Each week, design your pages for the next week. The steps below show you how to use your pleasure pad for writing your pleasure prescriptions.

STEP 2.

Know and remember the basic ingredients of pleasure

I have already provided sixty pleasure prescriptions for you to consider using in your own life. After taking several of these prescriptions, you can use them as models for your own prescriptions.

As you have read, there are three key ingredients of each pleasure prescription, so the first step in writing your own pleasure prescription is to gather those ingredients together in your mind. Here's a reminder of the basic components of pleasure prescriptions.

An *Aloha* Principle: The key element of a pleasure prescription is one of the five aspects of *aloha*—patience, unity, agreeableness, humbleness, or kindness.

A Briefly Stated Fun-damental: Remember that a fun-damental draws together an *aloha* principle and one of the aptitudes of pleasure—wisdom, virtue, or emotional intelligence—in a brief statement that helps you focus your mind upon healthy pleasure. Now, state your chosen *aloha* principle in the context of wisdom, virtue, or emotional intelligence. Remember, wisdom means calm reflection and maintaining a full life perspective; virtue means putting what you have determined through wisdom to be your basic morals and values into daily action; and emotional intelligence means being empathetic and in control of your emotions.

The Pleasure Prescription: This is a specific plan of action that combines the *aloha* principle and the fun-damental into a specific plan of action for your life.

You may wish to note this formula—*aloha* principle, fun-damental, pleasure prescription—down in your pleasure pad. Every weekday, spend a few minutes with your pleasure pad reflecting on the structure of your prescriptions. As you do so, ask yourself these questions:

▼ Am I wise enough to find the pleasure in my life by calmly reflecting, instead of constantly planning and rationalizing?

▼ Am I virtuous enough to focus on bringing pleasure into other people's lives at home, at work, and at play?

▼ Am I exercising my emotional intelligence by calming myself down and not allowing myself to fall victim to my emotions?

The next steps show you how to actually write your pleasure prescriptions, incorporating the basic ingredients described. Remember, on your Saturday or Sunday *aloha* review day, you can go back and rewrite one or all of your week's five pleasure prescriptions. Don't be afraid to rework and reshape any of your prescriptions. Leave a place in your pleasure pad to permanently record the ones you have pretested and found the most helpful.

STEP 3.

Get the pleasure perspective

Here's where the real creativity comes in. Only you know your own life circumstances and how much *aloha* you enjoy right now, so you are the expert on which of the *aloha* principles you need to work on, and only you know how it may be wisely, virtuously, and emotionally intelligently integrated into your daily loving, work, play, and healing. To craft effective prescriptions, however, you'll need one key tool—the pleasure perspective.

No one would want their pharmacist to rush through the filling of a prescription, to be distracted while filling it, or to not pay attention to the important task at hand. The same holds true for writing your own pleasure prescriptions. You have to sit down, slow down, and focus clearly on your prescription while writing it.

To do this, make time every weekday morning—before you get involved in the rush of the day—to do your pleasure-prescription writing. Even if you have to get up five minutes earlier to do it, set aside a five-minute pleasure pause every morning and, just as you might take a vitamin pill, take out your pleasure pad, sit down even if everyone else is hurrying around, and ask yourself this question:

"Am I living *aloha?*"

Look down your list of the five components of *aloha* as described above. Use the following questions to help you answer the question. You may want to write these questions permanently in your pleasure pad.

Would others say that I am patient?
Who would say that? (Write down that person's name.)

Would others say that I stay connected with those who matter most to me?
Who would say that?

Would others say that I am agreeable and pleasant?
Who would say that?

Would others say that I am unselfish?
Who would say that?

Would others say that I am gentle and tender?
Who would say that?

The pleasure perspective, you'll notice, means standing in another's shoes and observing yourself. By looking at your *aloha* from another person's viewpoint and writing down that person's name, you turn your focus away from yourself and onto your effect on the world around you. The pleasure perspective also helps to slow you down as you get ready to run in the human race by asking you to think about other people and your impact on them instead of thinking about how you are going to lead your own too-hectic life for more self-pleasure. Remember, healthy pleasure comes to you first and foremost from trying to make the world a more pleasurable place for others. Us-fulfillment, not self-fulfillment, is the focus of pleasure-prescription writing.

Taking the five-minute pleasure pause five days a week will help you start your day ready to live *aloha*. Again, remember to spend several minutes on either Saturday or Sunday reviewing your prescription pad and looking for changes in your ability to live *aloha*. If possible, do this with someone who knows you well, and discuss how you are doing. Are you more aware of breathing in life's wonders? Are you "con-spiring" (breathing together) with others in order to awaken to paradise?

After your five-minute pleasure pause, write your brief pleasure prescription for the day.

STEP 4.

Write it down

Now that you have your pleasure prescription pad designed, your *aloha* review day and delight diary established, the *aloha* concepts and the basics of pleasure-prescription writing reviewed, and you've set aside your five-minute daily pleasure pause, you are ready to actually write your prescription. Here's how to do it.

Each day, pick one *aloha* principle that you think could use some more application in your life. Next, write a simple fun-damental phrase to help you put that principle into your life context. Phrase it in a way that will help you remember to live that principle wisely (by being reflective, not reactive), virtuously (by walking the walk and practicing what you preach), and emotionally intelligently (by controlling your emotions and empathizing with others). Finally, write a specific behavior plan for implementing the *aloha* principle in your daily life. This is your prescription.

Here are examples of pleasure prescriptions for each one of the *aloha* principles. These were written by participants in my seminars who are learning the skill of pleasure-prescription writing. Notice that the three key statements that frame each written prescription are:

1. When it comes to living *aloha*, I need to try to be a little more ——

2. My life would be more fun for me and others if I tried to ——

3. Today I'm going to try to ——

Male accountant

Aloha Principle: When it comes to living aloha, I need to be a little more —— PATIENT.

Fun-damental: My life would be more fun for me and others if I tried to—worry less about always trying to show that I'm smarter than everyone else, and instead became a little wiser, thinking and reflecting more about what I say before I say it.

Pleasure Prescription: Today I'm going to try to—talk less, listen more, and pause and repeat what the person speaking with me has just said.

Single mother of four children

Aloha Principle: When it comes to living aloha, I need to be a little more —— UNITED.

Fun-damental: My life would be more fun for me and others if I tried to—get past my resentment of men like my ex-husband and be open to new connections in my life.

Pleasure Prescription: Today I'm going to try to—be more alert for and accepting of, and less cynical and critical about those who want to relate with me. I'll give them a chance without comparing them to my ex-husband.

Female surgeon

Aloha Principle: When it comes to living aloha, I need to be more —— AGREEABLE.

Fun-damental: My life would be more fun for me and others if I tried to—stop being in charge all the time and let others have more control.

Pleasure Prescription: Today I'm going to try to—listen more for other people's ideas and follow those ideas.

Female college student

Aloha Principle: When it comes to living aloha, I need to be more ——HUMBLE.

Fun-damental: My life would be more fun for me and others if I tried to—ask about others' accomplishments and lives instead of always telling them about mine.

Pleasure Prescription: Today I'm going to try to—ask three people what their greatest life accomplishment to date has been and how they feel about it.

Male insurance salesperson

Aloha Principle: When it comes to living aloha, I need to be more — — KIND.

Fun-damental: My life would be more fun for me and others if I tried to—be less "on" all the time and stopped seeing everyone as a potential customer and everything as a potential sales transaction.

Pleasure Prescription: Today I'm going to try to—ease up. I'll just be me, without regard for selling, success, or numbers, and I'll just try to get to know the people I'm talking with.

Now try it yourself. Write five practice pleasure prescriptions, one for each *aloha* principle, in the space below.

Aloha Principle: Patience

Fun-damental:

Prescription:

Aloha **Principle:** Unity

Fun-damental:

Prescription:

Aloha **Principle:** Agreeableness

Fun-damental:

Prescription:

Aloha Principle: Humbleness

Fun-damental:

Prescription:

Aloha Principle: Kindness

Fun-damental:

Prescription:

    I have worked with many children in writing their own pleasure pre-scriptions, and I've learned that doing family prescriptions together can be constructive and instructive. Here's an example of an eight-year-old girl's pleasure prescription:

Aloha Principle: When it comes to living aloha, I need to be more — — PATIENT.

Fun-damental: My life would be more fun for me and others if—people didn't ruin the game by trying to run it their way and yelling at the ones who mess it up.

Pleasure Prescription: Today I'm going to try to—take turns more and even let Tina play even though she is no good.

STEP 5.

Record and study the results

As you start to fill your pleasure pad with prescriptions, take one thor-ough pleasure review day a month that is not your weekend *aloha* re-view day. Go over your entire pleasure pad, if possible with someone who knows you. Look for which of the five *aloha* principles keep emerging in your prescriptions. What is your primary *aloha* deficit—too little patience, too little time and attention to your family or primary relationship, too much anger or hostility, too much selfishness, too much impoliteness or crudeness?

Once you have identified your *aloha* weak spot, start writing more prescriptions in that area. Look back as well at Chapter Four of this book, and check whether your prescriptions are incorporating the five ingredients of healthy *aloha* pleasure.

STEP 6.
Pleasure potential check-ups

As you practice writing and filling your own pleasure prescriptions, it is helpful to assess your progress by retaking many of the tests in this book and *The Pleasure Prescription*. Your score on the *Aloha* Test, found in *The Pleasure Prescription*, is a very good reflection of your progress, but remember, pleasure is not something you accomplish; it is something that happens to you and those around you when you pay attention to a life of *aloha*.

Now you're ready to start your pleasure-prescription writing. If your efforts ever cease to be fun, stop for a few weeks and then return to your prescription writing. Remember that shared and healthy happiness cannot be pursued; it must ensue from showing every day that you can deeply and sincerely care about the pleasure and joy of everyone around you. *Pomaika'i* (good luck)!

Hoʻomaka Hou (To Begin Again):
Updating Your Cheerful Navigator's Log

Pronounced "ho oh-mah-kah ho-oo"

I hope you do not feel that you've finished this book. I hope you will keep this book near you and keep going back to it as you write and use new pleasure prescriptions. You can use the next few pages to keep a journal of them. Remember, you've embarked on a lifelong voyage!

Before you close the book, update your "cheerful navigator's log" by going back to Chapter Two and answering again the three pleasure-prompter questions that started you on your voyage to paradise. How do your answers differ now that you've learned to practice and live *aloha*?

Do not be discouraged if you find pleasure-prescription writing to be a very difficult task. When you feel you are struggling, remember to repeat the phase above: *ho'omaka hou*—to begin again and again and again. Healthy pleasure requires that you see life not as a series of endings, but as an endless series of new beginnings. *Aloha!*

The Pleasure Prescription Supplements

Hoʻo Hawaiʻi (Speaking a Little Hawaiian)

The Hawaiian language is the core of Hawaiʻi's culture. It has the shortest alphabet in the world, but it's capable of saying much more with more meaning than most languages. The research of Hoʻala Hou indicates that, by just pronouncing Hawaiian words with respect and tenderness, one's blood pressure and heart rate lowers, stress chemicals decrease, and immunity is enhanced.

The Hawaiian language has only twelve letters. In very simplified form, here is a basic guide to pronouncing Hawaiian words. Remember, though, that respect and *aloha* are the keys to the power of these words and sounds.

▼ The vowels are pronounced *a* as in *father, e* as in *bet, i* like the *ee* in *beet, o* as in *boat,* and *u* like the *oo* in *boot.*

▼ The letters *p* and *k* are pronounced the same as they are in English, but with less emphasis.

▼ The letters *h, l, m,* and *n* are pronounced as they are in English.

▼ *W* after *i* and *e* usually is pronounced like *v.* After *u* and *o* it is usually pronounced as *w.* After *a* it is pronounced as *v* or *w.*

-An *'okina* (glottal stop) is treated like the pause in the English *oh-oh*.

▼ —A *kahako* (macron) over a vowel prolongs the sound of that vowel.

The *'okina* and *kahako* are not just marks of emphasis. They are key parts of every Hawaiian word. Because I am using approximations of Hawaiian pronunciation and trying to make the Hawaiian language easier to practice for those unfamiliar with it, I have left the *kahako* off the Hawaiian words in this book. I mean no disrespect for the sacred Hawaiian language by doing so, and I do understand that the words' meanings are much different with accurate markings. I hope my Hawaiian teachers will forgive my arrogance and ignorance in favor of opening the door to people who would otherwise never try to learn Hawaiian and encouraging their further interest in more meaningful, accurate, and respectful learning of this most powerful language.

Practice in *Ho'o Hawai'i*

Here is an *'olelo no'eau* ("oh-lay-low no-ey-ow")—Hawaiian proverb—to help you practice your Hawaiian. Again, use these words only with respect, tenderness, sincerity and gentleness. Remember, these words have very strong *mana*.

A'ohe loa'a i ka noho wale
Pronounced "ah oh-ey low-ah ah e ka no-ho vah-lay"
Distance is ignored by love

Take your time and pronounce each sound. By being patient *(ahonui)* enough to say the sounds slowly, connected *(lokahi)* enough to practice the sounds with someone else, agreeable *('olu'olu)* enough to make the effort, humble *(ha'aha'a)* enough to tolerate your own mistakes and the mistakes of others, and gentle and kind *(akahai)* enough to refrain from criticism of yourself and others as you learn, you are filling a most powerful pleasure prescription.

Glossary of Hawaiian Words

ahonui: patience, expressed with perseverance; the first *aloha* principle

'aina: the earth or land. Healthy pleasure depends on protective, caring respect for the land. None of us can be joyful if the earth is not happy and healthy.

akahai: kindness, expressed with tenderness; the fifth *aloha* principle

Akua: God

aloha: the key to healthy pleasure, meaning to love, to welcome, to care, to be patient, harmonious, pleasant, humble, and tender

aloha hana: working with love

aloha lapa'au: healing love

aloha pa'ani: loving playing

aloha pumehana: warm loving

"'Ano'ai ke aloha . . . ia kakou ah pau loa": "Greetings of love to be shared among us all"

E komo mai!: Welcome!

ha'aha'a: humbleness, expressed with modesty; the fourth *aloha* principle

ho'ala hou: to reawaken to the sacred lessons of *aloha*

holoholo: to joyfully sail and to cruise with life rather than trying to lead life

ho'olohi: to take things as they come, to take it easy, to slow down, and to accept the good with the bad

ho'omaka hou: to begin anew

kahako: a macron used over a vowel in the Hawaiian language

kaholo: the most basic *hula* step: step gently to one side, bring the other foot next to the first, and then move back in the same manner in the other direction

kahuna: a wise healer and spiritual leader

kalo: taro plant

kanaka maoli: the Hawaiian people

keiki: a child

kipona aloha: deepest love

kokua: help

kumu: teacher

kupuna: Hawaiian elder

lokahi: unity, expressed harmoniously; the second *aloha* principle

"Mae e holo ana": "Go with however it goes"

mahalo nui: many thanks

makaukau: ready

mana: energy, referring to the potent energy that resonates within every person, place, and thing

mauli ola: the breath of life

me ke aloha pumehana: with warmest regards

mele: a song, chant, or poem that expresses the *aloha* of past times

na'auao: wisdom, meaning connection, awareness, and respect for everyone past and present and for everything

na kupuna: sacred ancestors, meaning all of those who have gone before. They are within and around us at the present moment.

no'ono'o nui: to be contemplative, to reflect with respect on the meaning of our connection with everyone, everything, and every time

'ohana: the sacred family

'okina: a glottal stop used in the Hawaiian language

'olelo: to speak, meaning to respect and be careful in our use and expression of words. All words have *mana.*

'olelo no'eau: wise saying

oli: a chant or to chant, meaning to say Hawaiian words and phrases with deep respect for their origins and *mana*

'olu'olu: agreeableness, practiced with pleasantness; the third *aloha* principle

pa'ani: playing

paio: hostility

pauaho: out of breath

pomaika'i: good luck

pono: balance, referring to the sacred Hawaiian concept of things only being "right" if they are in the balance intended by the *'aina,* the *na kupuna,* and the gods. This balance does not refer to a single man's or woman's view of what is righteous, but to the natural balance of the cosmos—the way things are supposed to be.

po'ohula: to perpetuate the values of one's family

po'okela: working and defining success by values rather than by objectives

pule: prayer

pu'uwai: heart

'uhane: soul, meaning the core of one's being

Pleasure Bibliography

The following are sources referred to in the text and suggestions for further study for writing your own pleasure prescriptions:

Borysenko, J., and Borysenko, M. *The Power of the Mind to Heal.* Carson, CA: Hay House, Inc., 1994.

Dossey, L. *Meaning and Medicine.* New York: Bantam, 1991.

_____. *Prayer Is Good Medicine.* San Francisco: HarperSanFrancisco, 1996.

Dreher, H. *The Immune Power Personality.* New York: Dutton Books, 1995.

Goleman, D. *Emotional Intelligence.* New York: Bantam Books, 1995.

Hillman, J. *The Soul's Code.* New York: Random House, 1996.

Kohn, A. *No Contest: The Case Against Competition.* Boston: Houghton Mifflin Co., 1986.

Metcalf, C.W., and Felible, R. *Lighten Up.* Reading, MA: Addison-Wesley Publishing Co., 1992.

Miller, T. *How to Want What You Have.* New York: Henry Holt, 1994.

Moore, T. *The Re-Enchantment of Everyday Life.* New York: HarperCollins, 1996.

Ornstein, R., and Sobel, D. *Healthy Pleasures.* Reading, MA: Addison-Wesley Publishing Co., 1989.

Pearsall, P. *Superimmunity: Master Your Emotions and Improve Your Health.* New York: Fawcett Books, 1987.

_____. *Making Miracles.* New York: Avon Books, 1991.

_____. *The Pleasure Prescription: To Love, to Work, to Play—Life in the Balance.* Alameda, CA: Hunter House, 1996.

_____. *The Heart's Code.* New York: Broadway Books, to be published in April 1998.

_____. *The Pleasure Principle: A New Way to Health*. Six-tape audiocassette set with Hawaiian music. Niles, IL: Nightingale/Conant. To order, call (800) 323-5552.

Pukui, M.K. *'Olelo No'eau: Hawaiian Proverbs and Poetical Sayings*. Honolulu, HI: Bernice P. Bishop Museum Press, 1983.

Pukui, M.K., and Elbert, S.H. *Hawaiian Dictionary, Revised and Enlarged Edition*. Honolulu, HI: University of Hawai'i Press, 1986.

Robbins, J. *Reclaiming Our Health*. Tiburon, CA: H.J. Kramer, Inc., 1996.

Schwartz, T. *What Really Matters: Searching for Wisdom in America*. New York: Bantam Books, 1995.

Seligman, M.R. *What You Can Change and What You Can't*. New York: Alfred A. Knopf, 1994.

Senge, P.M. *The Fifth Discipline*. New York: Doubleday Currency, 1990.

Shaw, D. *The Pleasure Police*. New York: Doubleday, 1996.

Tenner, E. *Why Things Bite Back: The Revenge of Unintended Consequences*. New York: Knopf, 1996.

Here are two professional journals that contain cutting-edge research on new models of healthy balance and connection, and also contain the work of many of the researchers referred to in this book:

Alternative Therapies in Health and Medicine: A Peer-Reviewed Journal. Published bimonthly by InnoVision Communications, a division of the American Association of Critical Care Nurses, 101 Columbia, Aliso Viejo, CA 92656, (800) 899-1712, fax (714) 362-2020, e-mail alttherapy@aol.com.

Advances: The Journal of Mind-Body Health. A publication of the Fetzer Institute, P.O. Box 3000, Denville, NJ 07834, (800) 878-2997.

Index

....

**THE PLEASURE PRESCRIPTION: To Love, to Work, to Play
— Life in the Balance** *by* Paul Pearsall, Ph.D.
New York Times **Bestseller!**

This bestselling book is a prescription for stressed out lives. Dr. Pearsall maintains that contentment, wellness, and long life can be found by devoting time to family, helping others, and slowing down to savor life's pleasures.

Current wisdom suggests that anything that tastes, smells, or feels good can't be good for us. "That's plain wrong," says Dr. Paul Pearsall, a leading proponent of the relationship between pleasure, stress, the immune system, and brain chemistry. "Balanced pleasure is the *natural* way to physical and mental health, and the best remedy for the 'delight dyslexia' and 'toxic success syndrome' that are killing the joy in Western culture."

The Pleasure Prescription makes the connections between physiological research and "Oceanic" wisdom — the beliefs, customs, and practices of a 2000-year-old civilization. Offering an alternative to Western consumerism and Eastern inwardness, the Polynesian way is based on enjoying life and connecting with others. Balance, happiness, and health are achieved through the daily practice of the five qualities of "Aloha": *patience, connection, pleasantness, modesty,* and *tenderness.* This practice extends to all aspects of life — from loving relationships, parenting, and work, to healing ourselves and caring for our community and planet.

Slowing down the pace of life and listening to our hearts is crucial to leading happier, healthier lives. Pearsall invites us to embrace a new contentment and the compelling lessons offered here light the way.

"This book will save your life." — Montel Williams

288 pages ... Paperback $13.95 ... Hard cover $23.95 ... Audio $16.95

TO CONTACT THE AUTHOR

Dr. Paul Ka'ikena Pearsall presents lectures and lecture concerts and consults all over the world to medical, educational, business, and lay audiences. To contact him to schedule appearances or to order his other books or tapes, please write directly to his mainland office:

**Dr. Paul Ka'ikena Pearsall, Founder and President
Ho'ala Hou (To Reawaken), Inc.
P.O. Box 1632
Dearborn MI 48121-1632**

....

Hunter House
PERSONAL GROWTH, HEALTH

WRITING FROM WITHIN: A Unique Guide to Writing Your Life's Stories *by* Bernard Selling

Writing from Within has attracted an enthusiastic following among those wishing to write oral histories, life narratives, or autobiographies. Now in a larger format, with a new design and write-in journal sections throughout, it can help aspiring life writers to tell their stories clearly and vividly. Bernard Selling shows new and veteran writers how to free up hidden images and thoughts, employ right-brain visualization, and use language as a way to capture feelings, people, and events. He developed these writing techniques in the many classes he has taught over the years and presents them here in a warm, encouraging style. The result is at once a self-help writing workbook and an exciting journey of personal discovery and creation.

288 pages ... Paperback ... $13.95

MENOPAUSE WITHOUT MEDICINE *by* Linda Ojeda, Ph.D.

Linda Ojeda broke new ground when she began her study of nonmedical approaches to menopause more than ten years ago. Now she has fully updated her classic book. She discusses natural sources of estrogen, including phytoestrogens; how mood swings are affected by diet and personality; and the newest research on osteoporosis, breast cancer, and heart disease. She thoroughly examines the hormone therapy debate; suggests natural remedies for depression, hot flashes, sexual changes, and skin and hair problems; and presents an illustrated basic exercise program. Throughout, Ojeda shows how women can enjoy optimal health at any age with a good diet and nurturing lifestyle. *As seen in* Time *magazine.*

352 pages ... 40 illus. ... Paperback ... $13.95 ... Hard cover $23.95

RUNNING ON EMPTY: The Complete Guide to Chronic Fatigue Syndrome (CFIDS) *by* Katrina Berne, Ph.D.

Sore throat, fatigue, vertigo, headache, muscle pain, fever, depression — if you are unable to shake these symptoms you may be suffering from Chronic Fatigue Syndrome. Although it can be difficult to diagnose, CFIDS is a real, biologically-based disease with options for effective treatment and management. Written by an expert who has CFIDS herself, this award-winning book includes summaries of recent medical findings on treatments, ideas on living with the disease, and intimate stories of other sufferers. The accurate information and sympathetic, upbeat tone make this an invaluable book for CFIDS patients.

336 pages ... Paperback $14.95 ... Hard cover $24.95 ... 2nd edition

Prices subject to change

SEXUAL PLEASURE: Reaching New Heights of Sexual Arousal and Intimacy *by* Barbara Keesling, Ph.D.

First, here's what *Sexual Pleasure* is not: a general, use your fantasies, get romantic, light-some-incense, create-a-mind-set-for-good-love-and-it-will-happen kind of book. *Sexual Pleasure* is one of a kind. It starts with the first principle of intimacy: to experience deep sexual pleasure, you must explore your ability to enjoy — openly and sexually enjoy — basic human touch and relaxed, anxiety-free caressing.

This book show you how to fully appreciate the pleasure of touching and being touched. It takes you through a series of stimulating exercises done both with and without a partner to increase your sensual awareness and experience sexual ecstasy. *Sexual Pleasure* is unique because it encourages you to focus on your own sexual desire, rather than looking for ways to please your partner. Being more in touch with what you enjoy leads naturally to greater passion, greater sensitivity, and greater pleasure for you both.

Who Is this book for?

Sexual Pleasure is for everyone interested in experiencing lovemaking as a supremely pleasurable emotional and physical exchange, and in exploring the power of a deeply satisfying sex life. The exercises in this book can be used by people of any sexual orientation, and by those who may have physical limitations, or who are just learning about their sexuality — anyone seeking the secrets of strong and fulfilling sex.

Special topics include:

- **For women** — new methods on how to have orgasms more easily using your internal and external trigger points
- **For men** — how to prolong erections and synchronize orgasm and ejaculation for intense pleasure
- How women can have instant orgasms with their partner, or stimulate the G spot to have a "gusher"
- New masturbation techniques for men that will increase their penis sensitivity
- Favorite ways to play with your partner, increase intimacy, and achieve mutual arousal

For information on author Dr. Barbara Keesling, please see the following page.

224 pages ... 14 illus. ... Paperback ... $12.95 ... Hard cover $21.95

To order books or a FREE catalog see last page or call (800) 266-5592

MAKING LOVE BETTER THAN EVER: Exploring New Ways to Sexual Pleasure *by* Barbara Keesling, Ph.D.

Continually striving for new experiences and intimacy within a relationship is crucial to keeping the relationship growing and thriving. *Making Love Better than Ever* is for loving couples looking for sexual adventure within their monogamous relationship. In it author Dr. Barbara Keesling offers practical knowledge and rare insight about lovemaking in a warm, encouraging tone. Drawing from years of professional experience, Dr. Barbara Keesling explores the profound, complex, and soulful powers of sexuality. She explains that sexual exchange between loving partners provides all the elements for a happy, healthy life: touch, intimacy, communication, physical activity, and playfulness.

With the goal of improving this exchange and deepening the bond between lovers, Keesling provides a series of relaxation, body-image, and touch exercises that progress from simple to advanced. Some are designed to be done with a partner, some by oneself, and all can be performed by adults of any age, sexual orientation, and level of fitness.

Separate chapters discuss: how to have fun during sex; how sex can boost the immune system and even affect the look of one's hair, skin, and eyes; how to improve and maintain the physical toning necessary for a good sex life. Keesling's approach is backed by her work as a surrogate and therapist, as well as by anecdotes of real people's problems, experiences, and reactions, and topics clearly presented and explained. As she says, her book is "for people who want something more than just a sex manual. It is for those . . . who want to learn to make love in the deepest sense of the word — not just with their bodies, but with their hearts, minds, and souls."

Barbara Keesling, Ph.D., earned her doctorate in Health Psychology from the University of California and taught college courses for many years, lecturing on a variety of psychological topics. Her books include *Sexual Pleasure, Making Love Better than Ever, How to Make Love All Night* and *Talk Sexy to the One You Love.* She has contributed to or been featured in journals including *Redbook, Cosmopolitan,* and *Men's Health.* She has appeared on hundreds of television and radio shows including "Geraldo," "The Howard Stern Show," and "Real Personal." Dr. Keesling has been called everything from "The Martha Stewart of Sex" to "the first therapist who looks like she's actually had sex!"

256 pages ... 15 illus. ... Paperback ... $13.95 ... Available January 1998

Prices subject to change

....

SIMULTANEOUS ORGASM & Other Joys of Sexual Intimac
by Michael Riskin, Ph.D., and Anita Banker-Riskin, M.A.

For those of you who think "taking turns" is a fact of life, simultaneous orgasm can be liberating. It brings you into the moment — brings you and your lover into each other — and it focuses on the essence of your relationship and connection. For most couples, simultaneous orgasms happen accidentally, but with this book you can easily learn to enjoy them at will. Once you open the pleasure channels in your own body and become practiced at sustaining heightened arousal, then you will be able to come together anytime you want.

Sex, orgasm, and simultaneous orgasm in particular create deep emotional bonds between lovers. The program described in this book will enrich every aspect of your relationship. When your energies merge through the special vehicle of simultaneous orgasm, it will improve your communication and strengthen your commitment to and respect for each other.

Simultaneous orgasm is not only possible, but it can quickly become an important part of your sexual bond. This book, based on techniques developed at the Human Sexuality Center, outlines an easy-to-follow, step-by-step program for partners to become orgasmic, first separately, then simultaneously. It includes:

- New ways for men to attain the control that will allow them to have multiple orgasms
- Innovative techniques that allow women to have an orgasm successfully every time
- Partner exercises that let you experience every orgasm, even multiple orgasm, together

Simultaneous orgasm is the "great equalizer" in bed. It removes tension about who is going to come first or when they're going to come. Many couples report that it makes their sex lives more spontaneous and relaxed — and exciting! The skills that you and your partner will learn along the way will enhance your other lovemaking, from foreplay to post-coital embrace.

Michael Riskin, Ph.D., and **Anita Banker-Riskin, M.A.,** are both a married couple and board-certified sex therapists and former sexual surrogates. Co-directors of the Human Sexuality Center, they consult for hospitals and colleges in the area of sexuality and are well known for their innovative concepts and treatment methods. They live in Southern California.

240 pages ... 10 illus. ... Paperback $14.95 ... Hard cover $24.95

....

To order books or a FREE catalog see last page or call (800) 266-5592

ORDER FORM

10% DISCOUNT on orders of $50 or more –
20% DISCOUNT on orders of $150 or more –
30% DISCOUNT on orders of $500 or more –
On cost of books for fully prepaid orders

NAME

ADDRESS

CITY/STATE   ZIP/POSTCODE

PHONE   COUNTRY

TITLE	QTY	PRICE	TOTAL
Write Your Own Pleasure Prescription (paperback)		@ $12.95	
The Pleasure Prescription (paperback)		@ $13.95	
The Pleasure Prescription (audio tape)		@ $16.95	
Please list other titles below:			
		@ $	
		@ $	
		@ $	
		@ $	
		@ $	
		@ $	
		@ $	

Shipping costs
First book: $3.00 by book post; $4.50 by UPS or to ship outside the U.S.
Each additional book: $1.00
For rush orders and bulk shipments call us at (800) 266-5592

SUBTOTAL

Less discount @ _____ %

TOTAL COST OF BOOKS

Calif. residents add sales tax

Shipping & handling

TOTAL ENCLOSED
Please pay in U.S. funds only

(_____)

❑ Check   ❑ Money Order   ❑ Visa   ❑ M/C   ❑ Discover

Card # _____ Exp date _____

Signature _____

Complete and mail to:
Hunter House Inc., Publishers
PO Box 2914, Alameda CA 94501-0914
Orders: 1-800-266-5592 . . . ordering@hunterhouse.com
Phone (510) 865-5282 Fax (510) 865-4295
❑ Check here to receive our FREE book catalog

WYP 8/97